For

Steve and Eileen Scheel

&

Family

"Thought, fantasy, intuition, all are priceless heirlooms surviving countless generations. They provide no simple map, but rather a chart of finest tapestry, woven with threads of empirical wisdom by a thousand family weavers who walked before."

—Frederick B Scheel

Published in the United States of America by
University of Mary Press
7500 University Drive
Bismarck, ND 58504
www.umary.edu

ISBN 978-1-7348826-3-6

Design by Brady Braun
Printed in Canada

UNIVERSITY *of* MARY PRESS

A LEGACY OF PASSION

The Scheel Family Story

By Larry Woiwode

Overview of early Sabin, Minnesota, with future Scheels Hardware on the right of the street

COMMON CODES

A truth nearly universally known is that few family-owned businesses survive the second generation.

In the usual pattern, the first generation assembles resources and establishes a company, often in the family name, and the second generation, blessed by the success of the first, basks in the security of the business, vaguely aware of the dedicated effort behind the start-up of the company, and unaware that the same effort must be sustained if the company is going to continue to grow and flourish.

The new generation may lack business acumen, or undervalue the first generation with perhaps a tinge of hostility toward or disrespect for parents who seemed mostly interested in a company. They expect the income from the business to continue, as they travel to Europe, engage architects to design offices to reflect the company's status, purchase sports cars, a private plane—by now probably drinking too much. And when they realize business matters are not going their way, they descend into the state, as a businessman once put it, of being, "Penny-wise and dollar-foolish."

The family's business is doomed, and if that generation doesn't seek outside assistance or alter its attitude, the company goes under. In the best scenario, it's sold off to a huge corporation for half its value and subsumed into that corporation's holdings—or, as a member of the Scheele (as the name first appeared) family set the situation in a simple stanza:

Though oft repeated so none would forget,
Truth faded in time, the horrors and loss;
Saw life go on, heirs unaware of debt,
Lessons ignored as historical dross.

A telling refutation to the typical route of second-generation failure is the steady growth of the Scheele family company through five generations into the sixth. Across a hundred years the family has owned and operated a variety of stores, moving from hardware and general merchandise to a sporting-goods chain with outlets in thirteen states—a particular energetic burst of growth beginning in 1989, with the company focused on new vistas and innovative ways of organizing itself with each generation.

The Scheeles, like many successful entrepreneurs, are an immigrant family. The progenitor from Germany was Friedrich A Scheele. Also, in the German language when two vowels fall together, only the second is sounded, and "ich" is "k," so Friedrich is pronounced "Fredrick," or as a new middle-school student once said when he was asked to introduce himself to his class, "My name is pronounced Fredrick, but it's spelled "fried rich."

The Scheele family's dedicated motivation, common to immigrants, often overshadowed the settled population, with entrepreneurial energy obvious from the start. An additional consideration is that early immigrant families at the turn of the century, such as the Scheeles, had an honorable national respect for the elderly, the idea that Grandma and Grandpa could be as wise as any schoolteacher, while in mainstream America, beginning with the twentieth century, respect started sliding steadily south, as in the generational rebellions of the 1920s, the 1960s, and the even worse, dismissive, cancel-culture cruelty of the 2020s.

What are the avenues of success and growth that contributed to the longevity of the Scheele family and its company to this day? The answers include matters more profound than business acumen, as the generational wisdom and background of the business that became SCHEELS will reveal.

TO START

It's true that men, historically anyway, are formulators of the tenets of Christian doctrine and of ecclesiastical traditions that pave the way for a church's representation of faith. They weigh and measure and sift through manifestations of many doctrines to establish a logical working out of dogma the Bible appears to teach, knowing that elaborate verbal prayer can hold God at bay, while women often slip past all that into the profundity of faith. So it is that family history suggests it was Augusta, wife of Friedrich A, who influenced the cohesive Christian life the family came to enjoy.

Friedrich A was a mariner, a seaman who served, according to mixed sources, in the German Navy under the first German Emperor or Kaiser (meaning Caesar, King) Wilhelm I, or else, nearly simultaneously, under Otto Von Bismarck, Germany's first chancellor. Friedrich A anyway spent enough time at sea to bear the emblems common to that occupation—although in contemporary countries they're displayed by thousands across every level of the spectrum—tattoos.

While the Scheeles were in Germany, Kaiser Wilhelm I called for conscription into military service of all able-bodied boys, beginning at the age of twelve. Women are sensitive to subterfuge, the hidden motives behind the acts of men, and Augusta may have suspected Wilhelm I was preparing for yet another European war. He was, but didn't live into the twentieth century to oversee the war that surpassed every war of all time. His call for the conscription of German youth caused a massive out-migration from Germany beginning in the 1880s into the 1890s.

The progeny of Augusta and Friedrich A was Frederick M Scheele, their only son, along with a daughter, Margaret. For Friedrich A, the former mariner, this was his last voyage. At its end, he would be settled forever on the landed geography of a new continent, the United States of America.

Men are territorial, controlling areas they consider theirs, while women bear not only children but are rooted in creative truth with every step they take. Augusta was the prime mover in motivating the family to emigrate, since she was, as is true of mothers, zealous to preserve the safe life of her children—her motivation based on the fate of a son. It should be noted that she and Friedrich were Lutheran, a religious faith ingrained in the existence of the family. The Lutheran religion rose in the early 1500s and reigned in Germany until the end of the nineteenth century, and has been borne forward by the Scheele family for five generations into the sixth.

An elemental component of Christianity is the work ethic. Catholic monasteries from the sixth century forward operated under the concept of the division of labor, a practice abundantly clear by the twelfth century. Each monk or brother utilized gifts given by God, according to exhortations in Scripture. Those with organizational or administrative talents took on greater responsibility. In a perfect representation, the division of labor in a monastic community was based not on hierarchical status but on gifts of God.

Outside the monastery walls, the technical skills for a particular trade were passed from father to son, or possibly to the son of a neighbor. This was the general course of trade education in the medieval age up through the 1500s. No codified system of labor was established, so that specific occupations were not easy to know nor available for all to enter. That is why, with the rise of medieval cities, guilds were formed, and the guild pattern of serving as apprentice, then journeyman, and finally master, seemed the answer to professions that expected to attend to metropolitan needs. The guild structure, however, as with most, missed the mark.

Journeymen traveled to different locations, often distant cities, to carry on the skills of a particular trade they learned from a master. The master meanwhile trained apprentices who hoped to be journeymen, but at some point he had to travel to locations where journeymen were at work to inspect the quality of their labor and instruct them in further steps. There occurred at times, then, pauses in their work until the master appeared. And when he was away, apprentices who weren't traveling journeymen would practice basic tasks, over and over, and then wait for the master to return to train them in a new skill. In the 1600s, apprentices appeared in such regular attendance in London theaters of the era they were named "idlers." This system of labor, with gaps at each level, was designed to please a master.

FURTHER MOVES

The Protestant Reformation is often seen as ending a loose dedication to daily labor. A turn in the European concept of work began in 1517 with Martin Luther, nearly fifty years before the birth of Shakespeare—to place him in historical context—and Shakespeare died 160 years before the Declaration of Independence. Luther, Zwingli, and other reformers hoped for a general movement to alter the idea of work. Work, at whatever level it might be taking place, was not to advance a guild or administer praise to a master—an overseer or lord in the class structure that European aristocracy had established. For every individual now, work was dedicated, as in the monasteries, to the glory of God alone.

Luther translated the Bible into German, making it available to the general populace, and an unfortunate consequence of its widespread access was the Peasant Rebellion. The *Encyclopedia Britannica* states that the rebellion could "not have occurred without the impetus of the Reformation, specifically the incendiary preaching in towns and villages of Evangelical pastors who presented Lutheran and Zwinglian ideas as solutions to the problems at hand. The clearest evidence of the Reformation's impact on the shaping of what some modern scholars call 'the revolution of the common man' are the Twelve Articles drawn up for the Swabian peasantry by an Evangelical cleric and associate of Zwingli's. Article 3 of this document asserts, 'The Bible proves that we are free, and we want to be free.'"

That miracle of freedom allowed each person to work with his or her talents, given the opportunity, in service to God. It established the Christian work ethic, and brought a sense of individual liberty to peasants who were treated no better than slaves and saw themselves now as equal in God's eyes to aristocrats and masters. They were free of the levels of class or guilds—the guilds comprised of an artisan class that was a level above farm laborers or indentured servants. This Christian work ethic was carried from Europe to the generations populating America, where it gained a firm hold.

It held a special grip on a German Lutheran family who intended to make its mark in the New Country, as the Scheele family intended to do. This is apparent in a poem written late in life by Frederick B about his grandmother, "Grandma Augusta E. Krino Scheele"

Grandma was born to survive, with a Teuton will,
When immigrants came because this country was free;
Their gold was their thrift, hard work and a skill,
Making the least do as best, with a winning esprit.
I wish I had known her when she was a girl,

Wherefrom courage and freedom, the thrones in her heart,
Her self-reliance and faith, prized beyond pearls,
As each day's work was the morrow's head start.
There was little talk of such as principles of life,
Her family just lived them through hardship and strain;

Adversity was the forge tempering character from strife,
Beseeching God's grace, enduring the pain.

…

As I tend the family graves, alive with each year,
I picture her life victorious with her God,
I hold her in reverence, a true pioneer,
Her story of triumph, the long path she had trod.

Generational history holds submerged meanings at its center, and the same Scheele family member wrote in 1980 that a source of the distillation that "seeps into, collects and remains to stir each sense which comes down to me through the ages from the hunter and the warrior, the sailor and the seamstress, the farmer and the milkmaid, the merchant and the nurse, the artist and the artisan" is that very history's contact with the present.

He added, "Like most of our intelligence, our vision is the filament of our fathers and mothers for eons gone dark. Now again it is lighted through our eyes as we walk the road. What wealth of wonders awed them! What mixture of marvels and mates have fashioned the mental tapestries upon which our vision dances! What a miracle it is!"

A NEW WORLD

The Scheele family's first location was Chicago, a city central to the migration of Germans and Scandinavians who were sent, usually by train, into territories farther west. Western locations were praised for their bounty in extravagant advertisements in newspapers and posters and Land Patent brochures. A common promise, because of the general aridity of the west, was that rain followed the plow—false, of course, though a consistent claim in advertisements. We would know nothing of the Scheeles' time in Chicago if Frederick B had not included in the poem about his grandmother, this:

When first married, they lived in a hovel upstairs
In a part of Chicago where squalor reigned,
As Dad saw and would twenty years later compare
With what he remembered and what then remained.

That was on String Street where Grandpa worked
Twelve hours every day in the year but one,
Firing furnace for Swift when very few shirked
For of public health in that day there was none.

The "Dad" is Frederick M, the father of the composer of those lines, the composer his oldest son, Frederick B. What was true for the Scheele family was that its effort to spare a boy of twelve from military conscription, not to mention its dislocation to unfamiliar ground, gathered the family in greater unity. This ultimate strength underlies the Scheele family for generations.

Again, it was Augusta, according to stories and poems, who persuaded Friedrich A to move from Chicago. At this time Friedrich A Scheele

"Stormy, husky, brawling" — Carl Sandburg's Chicago, the Illinois River with smoky tugboats and cargo liners

dropped the 'e' from his name, perhaps because Americans pronounced it "Sheel-lee" or it may have been one "e" too many. From that day the pared-down name was, as now, Scheel. It was Friedrich A who initiated the tradition of passing on to the first son his given name, but with an altered middle name.

It's unclear whether the passed-on first name and initial added to family cohesion, but it was a leverage of tradition. The family unity and honoring of tradition allowed the Scheels to not only remain in business into the fifth generation, but to expand further in a creative sense, so that present generations emerge as the strongest in business acumen and innovation of any generation that has come before.

FURTHER UNITY

The countryside that the Scheel family moved to from Chicago was in Minnesota, outside the vicinity of Sabin. Sabin is ten miles south and east of Moorhead, Minnesota, its population hardly one hundred when the Scheel family arrived. The Scheels were Germans in a German community, and a local farmer had arranged—probably to acquire a hired man in Friedrich A—for the family to live on his farm. This farmer's family name was Proehls, pronounced *pearls* in its German permutation.

All Scheel children are required to work for the family from an early age, and in the year 1902, Mr. Proehls, who presided over his farm north of Sabin, gave three acres to the Scheels' son Frederick M and their daughter Margaret, and said, "Do with it what you can."

To assure accuracy, stanzas from the poem about Frederick B's grandmother reveal situations not otherwise recorded:

Later, after the family had grown to four,
They moved to a farm owned of German descent,
Where the two children grew potatoes to pay half the cost of a store,
Which became for the family life's turning event.

Frederick M, fourteen after the temporary stay in Chicago (although one account has him ten and his sister eight, which is doubtful) joined forces with his sister Margaret, twelve, and they spaded up the three acres for potatoes. They planted, hoed, weeded, and picked off potato bugs—a tedious and messy task if the plump bugs aren't dropped into a container of kerosene or solvent to prevent squeezing for the kill, their bodies bursting with dark liquid that leaves a picker messy after a hundred. Brother and sister committed to maintaining their acreage over the summer of 1902.

In the fall, the three acres averaged one hundred bushels of potatoes each, and Frederick M and Margaret sold the crop for one dollar per bushel. The three hundred dollars was conveyed as down payment on six hundred dollars necessary to purchase the first "General Hardware, Fred Scheel" store, as it was named in bold letters across its exterior.

Thereupon they moved into the back of the store
Where Grandpa continued endless hours each day.
In a few years they built a new home, and bought for
Income two houses to retirement defray.

The home for themselves was their reward in arrears
After a life of hard work, daily trials and no gain,
Their first decent house after struggling years,
Built on the edge of a village on a treeless plain.

She dug and planted a garden of foods she could can,
Tomatoes, cabbages, cucumbers, and beans,
Plus a raspberry patch, all part of her plan
To save all they could to further their means.

To add to the expanding vistas of the family—from Germany to America to Chicago to Minnesota—consider the liberating sense of accomplishment the brother and sister must have experienced in buying a building, an entire business location with their labor—or anyway providing half its purchase price for their father. That surely added additional family unity and a sense of involvement for the younger generation.

Now to draw a curtain open on the present, we discover Steve Scheel, a person of many talents, hospitable raconteur, the fourth Scheel generation to serve as CEO and President of the Board at SCHEELS, speaking to visitors interested in the developments of the Scheel family past as it relates to the present. He says, "I like it that my dad's poems are the best story—well, the only one—I have of my great grandfather and great grandmother Augusta. Yet, my dad regrets never sitting down and having a discussion with his grandfather. It's like that discussion I never had with my grandfather to find out what he did when he was a kid, what he liked when he was growing up.

"And so now, *my* grandkids, I make them sit with me and talk. I take them up to the cemetery in north Moorhead, near the sugar-beet plant, and show them where their great-great-great grandfather is buried, telling them as much as I can—though it's very little— about the generations and what they were like. They're all buried in north Moorhead. The grandkids do hear it, even though they don't seem to. My dad passed away in 2011 and every time we drive by the cemetery, a three-year-old doesn't forget that Grandpa is buried there. And then they want to talk about my great grandpa, and then it builds from there."

EARLY TIMES

The first Scheel hardware store opened in Sabin, Minnesota, in 1902, under the immigrant proprietor, Friedrich A. His grandson is Frederick B, and Frederick B is the grandfather the three-year-old continues to remember. Frederick B wrote of Friedrich A in a cascade of lines reproduced in part:

Grandpa's words were few but of a commanding voice,
His gait the roll of a sailor at sea,
The tattoos on his hand and arms by choice,
Branded men as tough as men can be.

Leaving home behind, he never went back;
Why was a question I failed to ask.
Like the ships he sailed, a trackless track,
Learning the life of the unending task.
…
Grandpa stood at seventy about five foot eight,
As sinewy as heavy work could weld,
With deep-set eyes, no glasses, a clear bald pate
And at maritime arts had long excelled.

There was no thought my entire boyhood through
To seek his story, his adventures learn;
Had he brothers? What did his father do?
Many questions which now within me burn.

What was his job when just a boy?
What was his school? Where did he learn?
What in a day gave him a touch of joy?
What made adventure within him yearn?

Frederick M, left, early on instructs a manager; managers are now leaders at SCHEELS

The Scheels were not loquacious, reserved to the point of few words, clearly not storytellers, as the questioning grandson reveals. Or were not so until Frederick B, author of those lines, began to open up with thoughts, practical notes, poems, histories—his own history and views of the family company. He eventually published a book of poetry and a pair of glossy, high-quality, coffee-table-sized books of fine-art photography. The first volume was gathered from his collection of nineteenth and twentieth century masters he admired (along with several of his own) and was first exhibited at the Plains Art Museum in Moorhead.

The interior of the first store, a croquet set up front, bicycles far back, and baseball bats lower left

Fred B, as he increasingly became known, wrote the first pages of a Scheel family-business history, and kept a biographical ledger of the main events in his life each year. The mariner, Friedrich A, seemed elusive to the Scheel family itself, with so few stories recalled about his life by any of the family, and, more pointedly, as the lines of poetry about him express, no questions asked. Most every detail of his past remains somehow absent and unexplained. It is clear, however, that he labored in the most thankless manner, firing a furnace for the Swift meat-packing firm in Chicago, in order to earn his family's passage west.

His grandson showed insight into his grandfather and the Scheel generations who would follow, however, when he stated at the end of the second stanza above: *"Learning the life of the unending task."* That is the self-employed businessman's code of conduct.

Horse-drawn wagons in front of the Sabin store, now with a facelift

HARDWARE, FARMWARE

Friedrich A's choice of hardware sales was, for its time, wise—a source of guaranteed income. Settlers and farmers needed tools and spikes and bolts and pails and pots and utensils and cream cans and animal traps and butter churns and scythes and hayforks and gardening tools and more, and that is what Friedrich Scheel sold. It may have been the perfect occupation for putting into practice a German adage: *Ein Platz für alles und an seinem Platz—A place for everything and everything*

in its place. A German-language expert weighed in and added that the more common expression in German is *Alles hat seinen Platz,* because "Everything has its place" was so imbedded in the culture its entire meaning was understood by all.

A striking photograph of excellent quality of the sort that will follow the Scheel family—two generations before Frederick B became a photographer—exists of the interior of the original hardware store in Sabin. The family lived in the back of the store, in neither comfortable surroundings nor bounteous space, as the tight-packed accumulation of

goods in the inner store suggests, and as those carrying on life in the back room experienced.

A photo of the store in its first incarnation depicts an adjoined retailer of General Merchandise, an enterprise owned, at one time, by F. A. Wyatt, whose name appears on its façade. All in sight is overlaid with snow smooth and crisp and even, including the street in front of an uncluttered frame building with two peaks, painted tan with brown trim—possibly a colorized photo.

The patriarch, Friedrich A, a lit pipe in his mouth, a seaman's remnant, and his son, Fred M, stand in front of the hardware store, along with a third person, Carl Buth (pronounced *booth*), manager of the General Merchandise portion, all three dressed in dark suits and exposed to the cold for the photograph, hands in their pockets. Recently carpentered entries of rough lumber, suggesting elemental woodworking skills, are constructed over the front doors of each store to keep out the cold. A small store of another sort clings to the far end of the building, its flat roof lower than the peaks of the main, which will serve as a further site of sales.

Friedrich A expanded the hardware store to include groceries and clothing in the Wyatt portion and smaller building. And soon Friedrich A began to sell small scale Deering farm equipment, such as single-bottom plows and two-row-checking corn planters, specializing in mowers and hay and grain binders. A bustling economy of the early 1900s is pictured in the number of horse-drawn wagons parked in the street outside the adjoined stores, where a spirited crowd is stilled in its action.

Fred B, the grandson who speculated about his grandfather, Friedrich A, wrote a forty-seven-stanza poem of rhymed quatrains that spills over into seven pages of small print, under the title "The Farm." Whether the poem is imaginative or based on a family-specific location, it is knowledgeable about rural life, and is quoted here in small-scale portions—first its opening:

> As cloud shadows pass and the sun appears
> Each leaf flaunts the green in her gown,
> While the drowsing owl rests in half dream
> Amid the vault of the great elm's crown.
>
> From his summit in life he looks down on the strife
> As it stalks the riverbend cove,
> And then away west to the Farm where its crest
> Stands out of a cottonwood grove.
>
> North from the barn lies a man-made lake
> Cradled in hillocks coarse-dug and harsh,
> Lake to river between, stretched vibrant green
> Lie the pasture, three fields and a marsh.
>
> …
>
> [Later, the narrator says]
> Out through the porch I spurred,
> Headed out where I saw the cows coming in,
> Hired Henry driving the herd.

Friedrich A, far left, Frederick M, center, and Karl Buth outside the Sabin store

Lowing and milling by the pasture gate,
Twenty shorthorns bawled out their wail.
Soon the barn was filled with the chewing of hay
And the hissing of milk in the pail.

Shortly teams in harness came in from the fields
To stand as if awaiting a call,
Until their harness was shed, bridle over the head,
Taken in and hung by the stall.

    …

[And he says of the grandparents]
Like conductors of their rural symphony,
On stage in home or the barn,
They directed the fields, the family, the work,
Key of B, Opus 12, called "The Farm."

    …

The farm of then is today no more
But the memory is blooming still,
Its vision roams ahead, beckoning me on,
Like curiosity when climbing a hill.

A sophisticated understanding of prosody is apparent, along with a technical skill superior to common rudimentary poetic efforts. The expression is simple, sometimes barbed with an ironic touch, as it pays attention to the natural world, all in phrases mostly unadorned and well-turned, rather than the sing-song swing and forced rhyme of pseudo poetry—a coherent and conscientiously shaped verse with a literary edge.

The notable dimension of his poetry, however, is that without it many of the incidents that occurred in the Scheel family over the decades would be lost, without any collaboration anywhere in the world of their existence.

SHADOWY WARFARE

It was during this era, when tillage and harvest with horses was standard, along with herds of hand-milked cows, as in the poem, that WWI was escalating with unprecedented destruction across Europe. Frederick M, the second Scheel generation, enlisted in the U.S. Navy. America was a later entry into the Allied effort—a horrendous conflict against the gathered Central Powers. The war took twenty million lives and left twenty-one million more wounded. It was called The Great War or "the war to end all wars," because the dead and wounded outnumbered the deaths of every war up to that time. It was not easy for a sane person in a highly educated, artistic culture to imagine humankind ever again entering into a war in the aftermath of that conflict that spread through Europe to Africa, the Middle East, the Pacific Islands, even China.

That Frederick M entered the war with no compunction suggests that the Scheels suffered no lost love for Germany, since the army he enrolled in was warring against that nation. And his position, since he was the one who earlier might have been conscripted at the age of twelve, may have been in part a desire to deliver payback, if that was the entire reason the family decided to emigrate in the first place.

In the photo of the Sabin store after Frederick M has returned from the war, in the early 1900s, when horse-drawn wagons and people in the street project a busy look, one can see, as in an early photo, a multilevel birdhouse mounted on the near, uppermost corner of the crown molding of the façade. The two stories of the bird hotel suggest it was fashioned as a Marten house. A Scheel interest from its beginnings in America was in avian life and nature in general, but especially wildlife.

Western Minnesota and North Dakota are the locus of a major migratory flyway of the United States, where bystanders to this day see flocks of birds so thick and numerous ascend in clattering noise from the Missouri River that it's unimaginable in the darkening cloud of flight against a quadrant of sky that not one strikes its beating wings against another. Wildlife in this abundance was a source of food for the Scheels, but they also acquired a sense of serving as conservationists, as shall be seen, and the poet already quoted says:

Wings gave the angels grace of flight to ply the hallowed halls,
To hover above the guilt of man heeding a higher call.
While wings awarded birds the miracles of flight,
Birds in turn awarded man invaluable insight,

Lifting their minds aloft, freed of earthbound thought,
To clean white clouds in endless blue, its untracked pathways sought…

It is said in Scripture, as Fred B knew, "The Son of righteousness shall rise with healing in his wings," along with the request to "Hide me under the shadow of your wings," in those untracked pathways he sought.

WINGING WEST

Following his return to Sabin from WWI, Frederick M managed the hardware and general merchandise stores for his father. But after nine years as local storekeeper, he may have begun to feel ennui, or restless fret, in the village of Sabin. Headway in business and life in general had to seem difficult to imagine, especially after experiencing Europe, and Frederick M put Carl Buth, known to the family as Charlie, and Chris Kuehl (*keel*) in charge of the stores in Sabin. Frederick M himself moved ten miles north and west to Moorhead—Minnesota's largest western city.

There he entered into partnership with Memfred Nelson, in a business the two named Moorhead Hardware. It was another beginning for Fred M, who obviously was competent to strike out on his own, though the stores in Sabin secured a financial base. He must have felt somewhere along the line a sense of satisfaction that his labor over a summer with his sister had been a support to the Scheel business to begin with. But as with most Scheels, then and ever after, his lips were sealed against self-congratulation.

In 1930, when America was beginning to enter the skids of the Great Depression, following the financial crash on Wall Street of 1929, Fred M crossed the Red River, a kind of family Rubicon, and entered the state of North Dakota. The city across the Red was Fargo, and Fargo became the city where the executive offices of SCHEELS were ultimately located. The offices remain in the city to this day, but have expanded to other buildings as the business has grown. In Fargo, Fred M bought out Swanson Hardware, on the second block of Broadway, and renamed it Scheels' Hardware.

His son Fred B, the poet, said of this time in a recording taped when electronic modes arrived, "Dad just stuck it out. He kept the expenses real low, and he took out of the business, I think, a hundred-and-fifty dollars a month. He gave that check to Mother and it was her job to run the family with that. A hundred-and-ninety-five-dollar sales a month, that's where we broke even on Broadway. You see, if we made over a hundred-and-ninety-five, why, we made some money—'Hay Fork, 85c, 8 in. electric fan, $1.69, 24-quart canner, $1.19'—and with one hundred we lost money."

A pursuit as engaging as their passion for business offered a curative effect on everyday reality for the Scheels—their passion for the outdoor life. Fred B said in the recording, "Dad loved hunting, even when he was by himself in his teens, his early teens, you know, down in Sabin."

In a photo of Frederick M, when he's the young man his son describes, he balances a shotgun like a yoke over his shoulders with a brace of five sharp-tail grouse tied and hanging from its barrel, and from its stock a single stretched-out jackrabbit depends from rear legs. The white building in the background to the right is the immigrant Friedrich A and Augusta's original house in Sabin; it stands to this day, after numerous restorations. Once the Scheels were settled in the land of 10,000 lakes, as the state's motto goes, their hardware store sold sports accessories, as an early photo reveals.

By 1910 the store had added fishing poles and rods and tackle, along with rifles (Remington .22 bolt-action "Targetmaster" at $5.65) and shotguns to their stock. If parents shied from the power of a rim-fire .22, a 500 shot Daisy Air Rifle was available for $1.75. These early fishing and hunting elements added weight to the eventual exit of the Scheel family from hardware into sporting-goods in the later twentieth century, a move enhanced by creative innovations that occurred in the twenty-first.

Fred B adds a statement to match a photo of him as he stands, a young man himself, beside a 1930s automobile with game arrayed over its hood. "I lived to hunt in those days," he has said, "because if we were going to hunt in the morning I didn't have to sleep that night." The attentive reader notices he doesn't say he loved to hunt, as he says about his father, but that he *lived* to hunt, a family passion carried into the sixth generation. The way the Scheel family work ethic endured was certainly related to an old adage, "You can't labor right unless you measure your leisure right."

EXPANDING FAMILY

From 1939 to 1946, Frederick M, bought stores in smaller neighboring North Dakota towns, such as Hillsboro, Fairmount, and Casselton. These were called "Farm Stores" but operated under the Scheel Hardware Company, and they "earned the loyalty of their customers," as a video of the history of the Scheel family states. Fred B adds in a voice-over commentary, "Dad had built such a reputation of keeping merchandise in stock, and finally the customers were saying, 'Well, better to go try Scheels first, because they'll have it!"

Fred B's older son, Steve D, says, "Dad one day came home with a 1964 Chevy station wagon with a kind of logo on the side—it was a bull then—a bull with horns, just his head, with print below that said,

> *Try Scheels.*
> *They'll have it!*

Another probable origin is supplied by Fred B's youngest brother, Robert, better known as Bob, who remembers the day his father told him to go check for an item in a competitor's store down the street. "I know they don't have it," his father said, words he delivered, one suspects, with a wry grin, "but see what they say."

The salesperson in the other store said, "No, we don't have it, but you ought to try Scheels. They'll have it."

Top: Frederick M Scheel with the bounty from one of his countryside forays
Bottom: Fred B with a brace of game on the hood of a car and in hand

Bob Scheel preferred lawn-and-garden and hardware to sports

Bob's father, Fred M, did carry the product Bob was sent to inquire about, and that experiment may be the source of incorporating the saying. The product itself is not defined in any family recollection, although a $7.95 tricycle is included in a visualization of the story, in a history of the Scheel family that has been organized and preserved in video form.

In Fred B and Charles and Bob, the third generation of the Scheel family was earthbound. The oldest, Fred B, was one of the few in the family who wrote about himself and others and the company in detail. Others submitted to brief interviews here and there, and that's it. The course of Fred B's life is emblematic in its diversity of outlook and interests, a true Scheel in that regard—besides being possessed by an inner iron resistance to the trauma of war and the kind of fears that cause anxiety and regret in others. He was born in 1921 in the Moorhead hospital, to Frederick Martin and Mabel Benedict Scheel. Their full names suggest that this Scheel would receive his mother's maiden name as his middle initial, while Frederick would continue to cling and remain.

"Neither my dad nor my grandpa were great people persons," Steve D says in a softer voice to a set of visitors who sit across from him at his desk. "They were financial wizards who loved numbers. I loved numbers too, was deep into them at every store I ran, but now I like to look down on them from about 10,000 feet. Dad said, 'It's fortunate, Steve, that you're a people person, because I'm not. People enjoy speaking to you. I didn't have as much time for people because I wanted the photography, I wanted the business, and that was it.' My father didn't spend much time with grandkids, and my grandfather never spent any time with grandkids.

"So I was fortunate," Steve says, "in that I was the oldest of twenty-four grandkids. I was the one that got to hunt and fish with my Grandpa Scheel. At that time I didn't think of it that way, but now I think, 'Man, was I lucky!' The other grandkids got gypped because they didn't get this time in a fishing boat, or out walking in the field with his German Weimaraner. It was fortunate that I was oldest of all of them."

Fred B was born in Moorhead, but lived in Sabin from his birth until 1927, when the family moved to Moorhead. An interest in photography started percolating in him in 1931, when he was ten, as he wrote in a

"Biographical Calendar" he kept and printed in the last three pages of his book of poetry. Three years later, his younger brother James, at the age of ten, contracted an illness that children struggled with before the advent of antibiotics, scarlet fever, and died of it in 1934.

Life for the Scheel family, as for most, was not a daily cakewalk.

Fred B graduated from Moorhead High in 1938, and from 1938 to 1941 he studied forestry at the University of Minnesota. He wrote that his "key journeys began with Dad and Mother's developing my love of life and of the realms of nature." The dedication in one of his photography collections is to "Mabel, my mother, and Virginia, my wife, who have always encouraged me, and Fred M., my Dad, who during my formative years drove me over thousands of miles of these great United States on adventures that lit the lamp that has never failed."

Fred B wanted above all in those days to serve as a forest ranger, to live in the woods and observe and maintain the beauty and manifold life brimming at every turn in the natural world. He wrote, "To see beauty is to walk into the wood upon that hill and down and out on the other side, leaving that beauty in the woodland. But to sew that beauty upon the inward eye, the dancing water-rustle of the aspen, the oriole and his clear-ringing song, stitching the treetops with garlands of orange, the lines and volumes of light that most please my eye is to never leave that woodland."

Rumors of another war were sounding above the beauty of nature, and Fred B, ingrained in American culture as immigrants can

be, joined the war effort as a riveter at Lockheed Aircraft in Burbank, California, from 1941 to 1942. His immersion in aircraft manufacture may have encouraged a passion for flight in this hunter who was an observant caretaker of nature—exploring birds in their flights and massive local migrations, the meaning of the multitudinous use of wings, as expressed in the stanza of poetry about wings and his concept of heaven and flight—all this magnified his lifelong inner interest and desire for flight.

Following the pattern of his father, Fred B enrolled in the U.S. armed services, from 1942 to 1946. He rose from Navy preflight training to fighter pilot in the U.S. Marine Corps and navigated an F4U Corsair in sorties across the theater of the Pacific. That theater included the Philippines, Saipan, Guadalcanal, Tarawa, and ultimately Iwo Jima and Okinawa. The general tactic adopted in the Pacific by the military was this: an elite Marine troop lands in an amphibious assault, after days of naval gunfire barrages; then, as forerunner and aid to the troops as they are landing, F4U Corsairs support the ground-attack by bombing and strafing the way clear.

The Battle of Guadalcanal, for example, resulted in nearly continual air combat for six months, involving pilots such as Fred B, as both sides, American and Japanese, sought to control Henderson Field, which was a launching point for aerial sorties. The field was named after an American aviator, Loy Henderson, who lost his life in the Battle of Midway, one of the first successful naval campaigns of the U.S. against Japan after Pearl Harbor.

THE FOCUS NARROWS

The same Fred B who earlier stood beside a 1930s car with game arrayed over its hood wrote of a curious experience that became the focus of his life over this period: "In the Marines during World War II, I purchased, or was given, four books: a book of Shakespeare's plays and sonnets, Bacon's *Essays, One Hundred & One Famous Poems,* purchased for a dollar in a store selling used books, and Will Durant's *Story of Philosophy.* These four books I carried overseas, and with a treasury of idle hours, both on and off the airfields, I read, then studied them all. Had I not had all of those interludes of vacant hours forced upon me almost daily, I wonder what my lifetime loss might have been, though certainly not as great as the loss of many comrades.

"Reading and rereading the four books, I enjoyed nearly everything therein, but the favorites were mostly poetry, commencing with Shakespeare's sonnet LXXIII, excerpts from his plays, and several works from the book of poetry. Most of the poems had a further reflective beauty in their strong invitation to memorize because of their rhythms of meter and rhyme. I miss this in most contemporary poetry."

This is from the "Introduction" to Frederick B's book, *Poems & Other Words,* 160 pages of poems, the "Other Words" a single prose essay in celebration of a visit to Tahiti and Moorea. Shakespeare's sonnet seventy-three compares the poet to a tree in the fall losing its leaves, its branches shaking against the cold where birds once sang, and this gives way to a sense of twilight turning to dark, which, the sonnet says, is "Death's second self, that seals up all in rest." The conclusion is a couplet that states, *One must love well what one must leave before long.* This may have meant to Fred the precarious existence of a combat pilot or the devotion he felt for brothers in his band, some of whom were not returning from their flights.

The poems were published in 2003, when the author tipped into each book a post-publication quarter sheet in order to add acknowledgment to Jerry Richardson and Richardson's wife Lou, both on the staff at North Dakota State University, who aided in its organization. He also expressed gratitude to Lourdes Hawley, who designed the book and carried it to final production after Fred B suffered a stroke at the age of eighty-two, as the tipped-in quarter sheet of 2003 states. Among the many arresting lines he recorded in 1998 about his experiences during WWII, long after he and all of America had celebrated its end, could be applied to a number of political and military situations in 2021:

> *Too few care to learn from those gone before,*
> *The long suffering maimed, given up to neglect;*
> *Defense scuttled for political score,*
> *For the hour's gain, oath and duty reject.*
>
> *Leaders free of the yoke of their one duty prime*
> *Let neglect sink until all's disrepute;*
> *Then all pay for leaders' short sighted crime*
> *With blood, limbs and lives until all grows mute.*
>
> *Suffering long after the last shot is fired,*
> *With wounds forever till life has expired.*

Frederick B Scheel with pilots and crews gathered on an F4U Corsair of the Marine Air Corps

The final line suggests a state of PTSD, as it was later defined, that many combatants, unlike Fred, came to suffer—or the effect a tableau of deaths can have on those who enter the gates of war in youthful promise and return home altered beyond their years. It staggers the capacity of thought to realize Fred B was able to retain through combat every essence of creative ingenuity he had from the start. He writes in the poetry book's "Introduction," that "Out of World War II, the decision within a year was to enter the retail hardware business with my Dad who had begun with his father twenty-seven years earlier." This is the first semi-suggestion that for him the borders between war, business, and creativity were all but non-existent.

The solace of solidity in working for his father may have helped the transition from air warfare to Fargo life. He would be the third generation to enter the ever-altering business of hardware sales. The

Scheels early hardware store on Broadway in Fargo,
dated by the automobiles present

Fargo hardware store would move a block on Broadway in time, only to occupy a larger space and eventually call into being another Fargo store. Fred B entered an additional note after his return from WWII, for the year 1946, in the "Biographical Calendar" he assembled at the back of his poetry book, where he registers the same decision of joining his father but with one added detail: "Entered father's retail hardware business while attending North Dakota Agricultural College" (NDAC).

Few who follow the North Dakota State University (NDSU) Bison sports teams are aware that NDSU was first NDAC. It was an agricultural college, a distinction meant to keep it from being confused with its competitor, the liberal arts University of North Dakota (UND) at Grand Forks. Students in the agricultural college, aware of how they were looked upon, even though a number of NDAC departments claimed superiority to UND, referred to their college with self-amused irony as "North Dakota Moo."

Frederick B notes in "The Calf Who Could Only Laugh,"

At the hour of noon he dropped out of the blue,
And his mother ran to greet him with tears,
While the great bull saluted with twenty-four moos,
And the largest headline in MOOS NEWS in years.

The name was changed to North Dakota State University in 1966, and few imagined then that in fifty years, in the early decade of the twenty-first century, the NDSU Bison football team would win nine out of eleven competitions for the National Championship of its division in the NCAA—the playoff games held in Frisco, Texas—and send three quarterbacks in a row into the NFL as starters or backup, while UND football wavered and dimmed.

The family's relationship to NDAC and NDSU prompted them to maintain, in the Fargo store and elsewhere, a section that deals exclusively in Bison sportswear. The buffalo-headed NDSU mascot, Thundar, sometimes appears at SCHEELS stores. And at the Fargo Dome, where spectator noise adds to the effectiveness of the NDSU defense, a see-through net to keep field-goal kicks from striking spectators rises behind goalposts when a kicking play begins, embossed across its center with huge letters: SCHEELS.

NEW DEFINITIONS

Fred B writes that he does not "recall having an interest in poetry during years of formal education. In high school we were taught about the works of some English and American poets, read a few of their poems and studied meter, but little that was memorable to me. When assigned to memorize a poem, many chose Sergeant Joyce Kilmer's "Trees" for ease of memorizing… The University was little different."

In 1946, Fred B married Virginia Jean Joistad, and at the same time resumed, in his words, his "active interest in photography." He also gave prose a try, his first effort a short story, which did not seem to satisfy him, or anyway has not survived. The next year his first son was born. It seems that certain parents, perhaps creative ones, have intuitions about a family member not only recently born, but on the way, and an indisputable proof of this child's difference from birth is that Frederick for the first time in four generations is dropped from Fred's first son's name.

A complementary moment in history occurs when a gathering crowd imagines Elizabeth will name a newborn after her husband, Zechariah, and she says, "No, his name shall be John," and the crowd cries, "But none of your relatives is called by this name!" That was how John the Baptist was named, and the new Scheel child was baptized in the First Lutheran Church in Fargo as *Steve,* though none of his relatives were called by that name.

The name is from Steve Douglas, Fred B's Marine Corps wingman—the pilot who protectively flies beside and usually slightly behind the lead of a flying formation. About that Steve Douglas no story exists, other than his combat closeness to Fred B, who may not have been able to speak about him beyond naming, because of the "great loss" as Fred wrote, meaning "the loss of many comrades," and could bear only to pass his name to a new life.

"I don't know the history," Steve D says, "I don't know what happened to Steve Douglas. But I'm glad I wasn't another Frederick!" In receiving the name, he was freed from what may have seemed a generational necessity. He was released, and perhaps received additional seismic uncoupling from the rigid metallic inventory and compartmentalized organization of hardware and houseware and lawncare products.

The uncoupling was obvious in later creative steps; these amounted to a half dozen decisions that opened wide the hardware business he had entered. The company motto he devised was an example of his outlook. He used it when he advertised for jobs at SCHEELS: "Do What You Love & You'll Never Work A Day In Your Life."

That was his day-to-day attitude, as he expresses it elsewhere in detail, and it led to his creating the triplicate summary of SCHEELS outlook: *Gear + Passion + Sports.*

MORE CHANGE

The same summer of his first son's birth, Fred B took on management of Scheels Hardware on Broadway in Fargo, the store his father Frederick M—the one with game suspended from his shotgun—oversaw at its first location so judiciously that he extracted only one-hundred-and-fifty dollars a month from the company for his wife Mabel to manage a household that had grown to two daughters, Kay and Pat, and three sons, the fourth lost to death.

Charles Scheel, brother to Fred B, also attended NDAC, and their father turned to a growing monetary interest that would become his vocation—working as a banker. With Fred Benedict back safe from the war, Charles soon to graduate from NDAC, and Fred B's first son, Steve, born, Fred M left the hardware business and became president of American State Bank of Moorhead. He had been director of the board from 1933 up to that date, and from 1947 to 1967 he would serve as president, and then as chairman from 1967 to 1974, when he would emerge as the largest stockholder in American State Bank.

It may appear that Fred M's association with American State was a source of funding for the Scheel family business that kept expanding after it crossed the Red into Fargo. But that was not so, according to Steve D: "The way my dad tells it is when he came back from the service in 1946, his dad said to him, 'You are going to run the business. I'm going to run the bank because it's not doing well.'

M emfred Nelson continued to manage the Moorhead Hardware that he and Fred M opened in partnership, and Nelson also became a partner in American State Bank. The Scheel family continued to maintain their residence in Moorhead that Fred M's spouse so carefully kept on her monthly budget. This, of course, was a matter of entire trust on the part of Friedrich M in the managerial abilities of his spouse, an equality not always present in America in the post WWII era. This sense of equality continues through generations of Scheels, and if women don't appear at the forefront, they're acknowledged at every step by those at the top.

In 1927, Frederick M's second son, Charles, was born, and in 1933 Robert or Bob Scheel—later sent to check whether a competitor stocked a product Scheels had on hand—was added to the household. The middle son Charles graduated from NDAC and became business partner with Fred B in Fargo. Fargo became the flagship location of SCHEELS as it grew and expanded to thirteen states, and its two-level store with a Ferris wheel not far from the entrance, along with

Charles Scheel

lifelike sculptures of presidents, besides restaurants and hangouts for parents, would eventually house the executive offices after SCHEELS incorporated.

In time SCHEELS became an employee-owned corporation, and in 2021 all of the executive offices, including 270 people who inhabited them, moved to a separate building in Fargo. Everybody except Steve D, who in December 2021 was a gracious host to a set of visitors while in the midst of moving to a redone office on the second floor of SCHEELS in Fargo. Now he was housed next door to warehousing space. "I want to stay here," he said. "I'm a retailer. I love the retail business!"

Fred B tried keeping a daily journal, a commitment that anybody who attempts this task, as Fred with his busy life did, is destined to abandon, as he abandoned it. He did, however, keep the journal-like entries he eventually printed in the last pages of his book of poetry. In 1949 his second son, Frank, was born; in 1950 he was elected president of the Fargo Junior Chamber of Commerce, and his first daughter, Rebecca, was born the next year, 1951.

He wrote, "Over the years, in business and photography, I have been alone on the road endless hours, which gave me further call, as I drove, to memorize poetry and fascinating excerpts from other writing, as well as spawn ideas for my writing. During the 1950s I started writing a few poems, most of which I did not finish until I picked them up some thirty years later." In his "Biographical Calendar" he dates the specific year he began writing poetry as 1954.

He was as serious about photography as he would become about his poetry when he returned to it in the 1980s, and set out now to become a professional photographer. In 1961 he attended an Ansel Adams' Yosemite Workshop, an incident that, as he wrote, established a "new and a serious turn in photography" for him. He added—to expand on his earlier statement of family history connecting with the present—how "a study of planes and patterns distills my vision and that distillation seeps into, collects and remains to stir each sense which comes down to me through the ages from the hunter and the warrior, the sailor and the seamstress, the farmer and the milkmaid, the merchant and the nurse, the artist and the artisan."

The complexity of that vision kept him occupied in his community, too; he was elected president of the Fargo-Moorhead YMCA in 1959; president of the Fargo Chamber of Commerce in 1961; and, in the example of his father, became a director of both the Fargo National Bank and Pioneer Mutual Life Insurance. As Fred M had aided his father in Sabin, Fred B and Charles, with the mathematical wizardry and backing of Fred M, began to expand the family business. They established new stores in North Dakota and Minnesota and, for the first time outside the primary boundaries of the states of its beginnings, in Billings, Montana.

That store was opened by Charles, and from 1952 to 1956 Charles was elected president of the family business.

NOT ALONE

Charles invited Bob Alin and Lloyd Paulson to join the company as financial partners when the business expanded even further. In the early 1960s the Moorhead store moved to a new location—its size doubled to 20,000 square feet. The newly-organized Scheels Hardware opened a second store in Fargo, and a new store in St. Cloud, Minnesota, which became the first Scheels Hardware to open in a mall, and by its location set a pattern for most of the Scheels stores from that day forward.

Over that decade Bob, the third son of Frederick M, joined the family business. He followed the example of Fred B by serving in the

Marine Corps as a fighter pilot, and then ranched for a period of time in Montana. He has written, "Growing up in the Scheel home in Moorhead was in fact being in the hardware business. We would go with Dad to the 212 Broadway Store during closed times and he would give us all jobs to keep us busy while he did office work. I always knew that someday I would be a store manager."

Bob graduated from Hamlin University in 1955—the next four years given over to the Marine Corps as a fighter pilot—and adds, "I went to work full time in the Scheels store in Billings, Montana, under my brother Chuck in October of 1959." Though Bob was ranching in the state after his service in the Marine Corps, he seemed to see the hardware business, the one he grew up in, as a better and certainly more familiar route to travel.

Fred B and Chuck were busy as partners. Bob says, "In June of 1962, Scheels purchased the Crane Johnson Hardware in the Southside Shopping Center in Fargo"—another address added after the original Broadway store. Bob and his family moved to Fargo to manage Scheels Hardware Southside, as it came to be known. This was an early store of the company located outside the traditional area of a main or a central street in a city or village.

In 1968 Bob and his family moved to Bismarck to open Arrowhead Hardware under the Scheel partnerships. He managed the store in the Arrowhead Shopping Center—not the Kirkwood Mall, source of greater traffic, where SCHEELS years later would prove successful—until it was clear the store would not generate

Scheels Hardware in Moorhead, 1962, displaying the Steer logo

enough business to justify its existence. It closed in two years. At that point, Bob returned to Fargo to become partner-manager in the newly remodeled 12,000 square foot Scheels Hardware north of the Southside Shopping Center. He managed that store and enlarged its space to 27,000 square feet.

He stayed with "Scheels Southside Home and Hardware" in positions of manager, partner, supervisor, and executive committee member until his retirement in 1987. He says his favorite memory is his association with wonderful fellow managers and employees, among the best people he spent time with. The caliber of employees was elevated to a higher level by another member of the family, who will receive credit at the chronological point when a training program he instituted occurs. In the mid-1950s, this person began working in the SCHEELS Fargo store when he was eight years old, stocking shelves. His name is Steve Douglas Scheel, the former SCHEELS president and CEO serving as host to visitors this afternoon.

FURTHER NARROWING

"By the time I was ten, I was supervising my brother and sister as we packaged nuts and bolts while sitting at an old wooden freight counter. The margin was far better if we packaged them versus buying them already packaged, and we were paid a penny for each bag. We could package about one bag every thirty seconds. My sister Becky would count them out, my brother Frank would put them in the bag and staple on a header, and I would write the description and price on the bag. In those days, it took three days to take an inventory of the entire place, counting all the nuts and bolts and every hardware item.

"Dad bought the old Merchants National Bank building at 122 Broadway, and on July 4, 1965, we closed the store at 212 Broadway and hauled everything one-half block south. I remember lowering the safe down the stairs with ropes and chains. Then we rolled the safe down Broadway to the new store and again lowered it to the lower level. We didn't hire any help. Just the regular store crew and some family

members did the work. We worked twenty hours and opened on July 5th in the new, larger 'spacious' 5,000 square foot location on Monday.

"The second floor of the bank was the Scheels advertising office led by Joe Pavicic and the bike set-up room besides. We would haul the bike boxes up the fire escape, set them up, and then bring them to the basement bike shop. By the time I was twelve I was setting up trikes, bikes, and wash tubs in the basement. The ceiling under the 122 Broadway store was less than six feet high so we had trouble moving things around and couldn't stack much. But it was far better than the basement at 212 Broadway. It had windows and no dust. We had Speed Queen washers and dryers in the basement along with a Toyland and our service shop.

"In the early 1960s, Dad would drive to Breckinridge, Minnesota every Thursday to help the store manager and often I would ride along to talk about everything from business to wildlife. We had a 1956 Ford Station wagon and often hauled merchandise as well. Dad held 'Management Candidate Meetings' every Friday morning at the customer service counter at 122. About fifty percent of the candidates failed or quit the first year, but a few others and I survived the lessons and the business for long careers."

In 1972 Steve for the first time stocked athletic or running shoes. The brand of shoes was Blue Ribbon, an early name for a company that was to become Nike. The shoe that Steve hoped SCHEELS stores would carry in 1972, when sports clothing and shoes were being added to the stores' stock, was the brand most popular at the time: Adidas. But Adidas refused to let "a hardware store" carry its shoes.

The 1972 breakthrough with shoes led Steve D to suspect the ultimate transformation of Scheels should be from a hardware store to a purveyor of every type of sporting good, every style of sporting shoe and all sporting clothes for every sport, along with every type of sports equipment. If analogues are helpful, the first Scheels stores resembled a True Value or Ace Hardware, but included many everyday essentials for a time when no electricity or hot-and-cold running water was available, not till the 1950s, in the geographical area of the first stores. For the next Scheel move into light farm equipment and farm supplies, the comparison might be TSC or Runnings. SCHEELS was catching up with its primary competitors in the business, Cabela's and culturally-sensitive Dick's.

In the meantime, the investors Bob Alin and Lloyd Paulson heightened a generosity present in the Scheel family in their entry into the business. The beginnings of the two were different. Alin responded to an ad in the Fargo Forum that Fred B, former Marine, placed; it ran: "Learn Hardware Management; Become a Scheels Hardware Manager." Fred B hired Alin and gave him his first job at the store located at 212 Broadway in Fargo.

From 1956-1962, Alin was in sales, while also serving as a manager trainee. Near the end of that time he became not only the manager of Scheels Hardware when it moved one block to 122 Broadway, but a business partner with the Scheel family itself. This is one of several examples of the family being neither exclusionary nor self-centered, but invitational.

What Alin liked best about his job, he said, was working with Fred B to train managerial candidates. He was involved in community organizations such as the Service Club, the Chamber of Commerce—where he served on the board of directors—and as vice chair of the United Way Campaign. He additionally spent fourteen years in the North Dakota National Guard, two of them on active duty during the Korean War, and reached the grade of First Lieutenant.

He encouraged the Scheels in their support of Dollars for Scholars, an organization that awards scholarships to deserving college students, and they continue that ministry to this day. He worked out a plan to establish twenty-five Dollars for Scholars chapters across North Dakota and, that done, he turned to the Herculean effort of establishing fifty more, and then established yet more in the state of Montana. He organized the effort to build a new central office in North Dakota for the Dollars for Scholars organization, and through the 2000s to today, 465 Dollars for Scholars Chapters are in operation nationwide. Alin was instrumental in this growth.

WIDE TENT

Lloyd Paulson, another significant employee, "an early leader," as Scheels' records refer to him, said he was working at

Bob Alin,

who expanded the outreach of
Dollars for Scholars

Lloyd Paulson,

along with Bob Alin, increased the
legacy of SCHEELS charitable nature

Steve Hulbert

worked up from a dollar-an-hour job to
member of SCHEELS executive committee
and president

another hardware store but knew Scheels was the most progressive (to use his exact words), which led him to apply for a job. Charles hired him and placed him in sales at the Fargo store on 212 Broadway. In early 1955, when Charles left to manage the store in Billings, Montana, Lloyd became manager of yet another purchase by the partner brothers: Erickson-Hellickson-Vye Hardware in Wheaton, Minnesota, now a SCHEELS store. In that transition Paulson became a partner with Fred B and Charles, as Bob Alin had, and in his first year at Wheaton, Paulson raised sales to $170,334, a huge figure for the fifties, with a profit on sales of $18,505, meaning a 26.8 percent net profit return.

Lloyd went on to manage Scheels Hardware in Moorhead, seeing first to the construction of a 20,000 square foot building composed of a new exterior material—exposed aggregate on pre-stressed concrete, as a photograph illustrates. It was Lloyd Paulson who was influential in introducing not only the Scheels but Bob Alin himself to Dollars for Scholars.

SCHEELS gave and continues to give to communities where its stores are located, and contributes to other religious, community, and local and national causes, besides the Dollars for Scholars and the United Way, including the Salvation Army, First Lutheran Church, the Jeremiah Project, the University of Mary, Friends of the Children, and also the ministerial organization assembled and sponsored by one of NDSU's most memorable quarterbacks, Carson Wentz, who now quarterbacks in the NFL.

The work of Alin and Paulson helped enhance the legacy of community service embedded in present-day SCHEELS stores, from the Dakotas to Colorado and Iowa and Utah and Texas and Nevada, where each store gives at least five percent of its profits in contributions to the local community, although the success of the stores often motivates them to increase charitable contributions to ten percent of profits, out of gratitude.

Bob Scheel, for instance, after he retired and moved with his family to California, stayed in touch with SCHEELS to the degree of keeping a cottage at Pelican Lake, Minnesota, near the North Dakota border. In 1999 he became interested in The God's Child Project out of Bismarck. "Its main mission is located in Guatemala," he says, "and since 2002 we have been traveling to Guatemala every year as part of their Service Teams." He became fully involved with the program, he says, when he was installed as the Bismarck God's Child Board President, which has turned into a nearly full time job. "We look forward to many rewarding years with our involvement in this project," he says.

SCHEELS was formed as an incorporated company in 1969, although all the partnerships weren't yet converted into one corporation. In that year of Woodstock and further revolutions of the sixties, the Scheel family held firm. One of the company employees, Steve Hulbert, was starting to step up the company ladder. He had started at SCHEELS because of better hours and better pay, he stated. After working nights for a dollar an hour, the minimum wage of the era, he started at Scheels for a dollar fifteen.

If an additional fifteen cents an hour doesn't seem a record-breaker, remember that a 500 shot Daisy Air Rifle of the era sold for $1.75. The additional fifteen cents over a forty-hour week would garner him an extra six dollars each week, a relative bounty in the day. He worked at the main store, as it was called then, in Fargo, cutting rope and chains, mastering house keys, mixing paint—everyday customer service of the sort that all members of the Scheel family took part in.

Hulbert became a full-time hardware salesman and tool department manager, and then a gun and sports manager, as increased elements of sporting supplies were added to Scheels stores. Soon Hulbert was an assistant manager and then a manager candidate. Then the important appointment arrived; it was reported in a newspaper article that Fred B and Charles P, partners in "Scheels Hardware and Sporting Goods," had solidified arrangements to open a store in the Madison East Shopping Center in Mankato, Minnesota. The new store was scheduled to open the day after Thanksgiving. It would be the ninth store of the partners in Minnesota, North Dakota, and Montana.

For Steve Hulbert, it would be the first store he would manage, after serving as assistant manager of Scheels in Fargo. While Hulbert was employed by Scheels, he was also attending NDSU, but planned to arrive in Mankato with his wife and two children in early October. He had moved to a managerial position thanks to the inclusive nature of the Scheel family for a person who once worked nights at a gas station for a dollar an hour. And that was only the start.

On October 1, 1974, all the Scheel partnership stores were converted into one corporation with Charles Scheel as president.

NEW TRENDS

Hulbert became the initiating manager of Northside Scheels at 15th Avenue North and Broadway in Fargo. The building was a former Red Owl grocery store. A report in the Fargo Forum for March 29, 1975, noted that "Red Owl plans to move in June. At that time, Scheels will renovate the present Red Owl buildings for a hardware and sport shop. Current plans are to have the new store open Oct. 1

"The major departments in the store will be hardware service, sports, lawn and garden and housewares. The sports store will include a full bicycle repair shop… The new store will be the Scheels' fifth in Fargo-Moorhead, and 13th in Iowa, Minnesota, North Dakota, and Montana. It will be the sixth store in North Dakota, as there currently are three stores in Fargo and one each in Bismarck and Minot."

In 1976 Steve Hulbert became an executive committee member. One of his favorite activities when he was working and managing for SCHEELS was the Hardware Convention in Minneapolis, where products had to be ordered, generally twice a year, to keep the growing number of stores supplied with the newest products to establish those eight-weeks of in-store stock. Several company photographs record the participants at the hardware convention events, where the necessary ordering of stock was maintained.

In the late sixties Fred B attended his second Ansel Adams' Yosemite Photography Workshop, although he continued to remain locally engaged. He was elected to the 1972 North Dakota Constitutional Convention, and that year soloed in his first flight

SCHEELS STORE MANAGERS – 1981
Top: Bob Foslein, Ron Baldwin, Steve Hulbert, Gary Manea, Bill Joens, Dennis Reed, Steve D. Scheel, Ross Johnson
Bottom: Greg Haux, Bob Scheel, Wally Melchior, David Revier, Tim Gette, Bob Alin, Bob Bergeman, Bill Walker

Fred B with his beloved Pitts aerobatic stunt plane

since WWII. No record exists of the type of aircraft engaged for his solo flight. It may have been a fighter-type or acrobatic plane, because in 1975 he notes that he "purchased a Pitts S-I-S aerobatic plane and began 22 years of acrobatic flying."

The aircraft was designed by Curtis Pitts, a favorite for years of pilots who demanded speedy acrobatic maneuverability. It could climb 2,700 feet per minute, roll 300 degrees per second, and it won more acrobatic contests than any aircraft in U.S. history. It also broke records, including ninety-eight inverted flat spins (which means revolving the plane 360 degrees while hanging upside down) beginning at 20,000 feet down to 2,000, too low for comfort, and the plane won the U.S. Acrobatic team a World Championship in 1972. That may have led to Fred B's purchase.

His son, Steve D, notes about the Pitts planes, "They were custom-built in Afton, Wyoming. I remember he went out to get it and flew it home, and when he flew up in that plane, that was about as happy as I've ever seen him. That plane, he just loved that plane, and then he sold it on his 75th birthday. Too many of his friends were getting killed in those Pitts."

It was neither a sleek nor attractive aircraft, a short stout biplane with—to examine Fred B's prototype—large letters of N8FS inscribed on the side of its white-and-red striped fuselage. In a photograph from the time, Fred B stands in its open cockpit, presenting to the viewer a perspective on its pared-down size and shipshape design.

LIVING IT

The fourth Scheel generation, Steve D, after working in family stores, attended St. Olaf College in Northfield, Minnesota, where he earned a triple major in economics, political science, and history. And then, as with most Scheels, he served in the armed forces as an Army combat engineer. He was the oldest son of Fred B, aware of his father performing in his acrobatic stunt plane at aerial shows. That may have seemed at times an analogue to the insights and experimental potentials he was carrying even then in his head.

All the delights of the stunts a pilot can experience in the air, as recorded in a five-page-long poem, can be visited for those who don't turn semi-conscious when flying upside down:

Finding we are in the sky alone
We pull vertical, spinning slowly right,
Cartwheel over and down again
With a YAHOO! of delight.

Levelling out, we pull up in a half loop
Until hanging on the belt,
And around the loop is finished
As the tracking bump is felt.

Next we bore into a snap roll,
A blurring horizontal spin,
With a flick of the stick and rudder,
We whip around and level again.

...

We balance to hold the vertical
As we slide back tail first,
Until whipped around and headed down,
Rather instantly reversed.

Bays in the clouds beneath us
Open to caverns of Earth below,
Rolling up and over and down,
Into the nether world we go.

We pull up again into a half loop,
Stalling inverted at the top,
Push the stick full forward
And left rudder to the stop.

Slowly into an inverted spin
I watch the wings rotate,
Until I add a touch of throttle
To flatten and accelerate.

After a half dozen rotations
I push right rudder to the stop
To slow and halt the whirling
Until we enter a vertical drop.

And so he goes for four-and-a-half more pages, advisable only for any who enjoy linguistic vertigo. A new art, this one more adventurous, was added to Fred B's imaginative capabilities. He was also on the road over many hours for the company, as he mentions, driving a gravity-dependent automobile. Over that time, he memorized the poetry of others and received or jotted down lines of his own, almost all of which he did not look at or rewrite until the 1980s into the 1990s—a complicated process visited later.

On one of these business trips to the far south, in Louisiana in 1966, with his wife Virginia along in the car, Fred passed a rural service station with several men standing in poses that looked so photographically appealing to him he felt he had to turn around and go back and get a photo of the pattern of arrangement he'd glimpsed.

Virginia said, "Don't you dare!"

But he got out of the car and walked back to the service station. He had heard about and perhaps met Red-Tail fighter pilots, as they became known, from Tuskegee Institute, whom the military allowed to join Army pilots near WWII's end. No matter how Virginia or Fred felt about it, it was an artistic opportunity. He was not a people person, but had to be pleasant and perhaps smiled like his son Steve. He met the fellow who was the boss, Bully London, and asked if the half dozen

Bully London and Friends
Rural Crossroads General Store near Jackson, Louisiana   ca. 1966

men would mind arranging themselves as they'd been moments ago, when he drove by. He probably held up his 4x5 Graflex, credited for the picture.

Bully London seemed to feel they could accommodate the photographer, so Fred likely used a tripod for his Graflex, whose bellows extended as a form of focus while he looked at a rear image projected on glass. The Graflex was one of several cameras he carried as he traveled, along with a sophisticated 35 millimeter, the choice of news photographers.

The portrait is remarkable in its arrangement and perspective, the near corner of the service station drawn slightly closer to the observer, so that Bully London, standing enigmatically to the right with the bill of his cap at a tilt, hands at his sides and legs slightly parted, planted as if at the ready for whatever might arrive, is unaware of two fellows to the far left of the composition, one standing, one squatting, who stare toward London, singling him out, (including one way back against the building), as the artistic focus of the frame.

The photograph, along with others by Fred B, first appeared in the coffee-table book, *A Search to See.* It is gathered with others at the center of this volume as a recreational pause for readers to rest their eyes and relax by entering the perspective of another dimension. The photographs examine a variety of landscapes, from the United States to Mexico and South America and Europe and countries farther afield. They include photos of Fred B's that appeared along with Ansel Adams, Henri Cartier-Bresson, and other prominent graphic artists in *A Search to See,* the first of the two books Fred B published. In *A Search to See II,* he is the single photographer, and some of his portraits of people are so exact it's as if you're looking inside the person his camera memorialized. He developed his own photographs in darkrooms he built. The introduction to *A Search to See II* is included as a separate addendum at the end of this book, for its remarkable insights into related forms of expression.

NO PHOTO

It seems safe to say that in the general sense of a son who started working for his father when he was eight, Steve admired his father for his accomplishments, not only as a businessman but as an artist in more fields than one. However, Steve would not neglect to mention that a missing element in the life of others was a grandfather's touch; the lack of attendance of Fred B at school activities Steve's children were involved in. When Steve considered the travels of his father on "many photography trips to Europe and Africa," as Fred B put it, it seemed he could have traveled locally to attend the athletic and music events of Steve's children. Steve says he remembers his father visited three of the events his children were involved in when they were in school.

"That was about it," he said. "He enjoyed it when my son Steve Michael gave a saxophone solo at the front of the stage. I'm sure glad Dad was there because when Steve was done with the solo Dad was the first one who stood up and started clapping. Then the rest of the house followed suit.

"But that was rare. I played football, track, and hockey at St. Olaf College and my dad came to the last hockey game of my senior year. It was photography, it was business, it was traveling; and he got that acrobatic plane a little later, after I graduated from college, in 1975."

It's not clear to what degree this may have rankled Steve, since he spent many hours on business and traveling, and became the coach of Squirt and Pee Wee Moorhead hockey teams. "I took a five-hundred-dollar-a-month cut and came to work for Dad because he's such a good salesperson," Steve says. This was after Steve noticed that big box stores and chains such as Lowe's were opening across the country, compounding the competition to stores in hardware and houseware. "The profits for houseware and hardware are about the same, but sporting goods average a much higher retail price, so a ten-dollar profit on water skis adds up faster than a nickel or dime on a handful of nails," Steve adds.

He acknowledges his father as a creative font, free from generational traditions, and admits he inherited both a love of numbers and a creative strain from his father, along with a sense of daring. But the focus of Steve's creative energy entered the heart of the family company. He added to its expanding stores innovative ideas never before seen in sporting goods, much less most retail establishments. At that moment in time, remaining as courteous as he could to a father who resisted being a grandfather, he may not have been able to focus his vision as one focuses a camera, much less clearly enunciate the direction of the vision he awakened with each day.

Fred B's endeavors were grounded in a gift for precision and control, whether finding the perfect framing of a person, object, or ensemble he hoped to capture on film, or the combination of using every extremity (not to mention cold-hearted courage) in performing the stunts for real that he rendered in stanzas about his N8FS Pitts acrobatic plane. Gifts of his caliber can tempt a person to leverage that kind of control over external events with a similar assured artistry—a calibrated control defined by an ingrained knowledge of the limits of external reality, as a pilot learns those, set in the existential reserve combat veterans exercise in order to endure stateside lives of domesticity, meaning life itself.

But perhaps that attitude occurs only if a chink of insecurity exists in the intellect. In the 1970s a moment arrived when the gifts of father and son seemed in collision with each other, almost as if, *Which would win?*

TEMPEST IMPASSE

According to Steve D, "I remember my dad would say, 'If you think that's the right thing to do, do it.' I never asked my dad for anything because I was like my son, Steve Michael, who never asked *me* for anything, except when he was struggling at UND, when it was financially—'Put me through one year,' he said, 'I want to prove I can do it!'

"I'd walk into my dad's office on a fairly regular basis—mine was next door—and say, 'Dad, what do you think?'—about an idea I had.

He'd never tell me. He'd say, 'What do you think?' So I'd tell him what I thought, and he'd say, 'Just do it.'

"The only time he didn't give the go-ahead was in 1976 when I was moving down to Sioux Falls to open our first store in South Dakota. I walked up to his desk—he had a pretty Spartan office—and asked if I could make that store all sporting goods.

Modern, graceful lines of a store when sports began to be a mainstay

"His fist came down on the desk so hard everything must have jumped a half inch. He said, 'The first thing people can do without is sporting goods! That will be hardware, housewares, lawn and garden, and sporting goods—in that order!'

Storewide research by then revealed that nearly fifty percent of the income of SCHEELS derived from sporting goods. Steve believed SCHEELS had to undergo an entire sporting-goods shift to survive and prosper. His father was CEO of the hardware and homeware stores in a four-state region, and Steve, now thirty, was in his fifth year of working for the company. He had after all given up five-hundred dollars a month to move to SCHEELS.

"I'd been in the Army," he recounts. "It was a volunteer Army, and I was getting out in 1971, but before that happened my wife and I managed an apartment complex in Colorado Springs. We lived off post. We got free room and board because of the apartments. I got paid by the Army, and I worked part-time at Dave Cook's Sporting Goods"—a link to the direction he would travel—"in downtown Colorado Springs."

"Dad said I should come back and try the business. I really wanted to be a teacher and a coach, and he said, 'Well, you can be a teacher and a coach in the business, too.'"

Steve did become a teacher in the later training sessions he instituted. And he got to coach, too. He coached the Moorhead Squirt and Pee Wee hockey team for sixteen years. He did that in the midst of all that was going on. "And I get to teach and coach still to this day, *in the business*," he says, "and I so enjoy it!"

His first major out-of-state assignment was opening the store in Sioux Falls. Fred B was the third generation to deal in hardware—necessities, as he saw it (which was true) to people living and working in the agricultural areas where Scheels Hardware stores were mostly located. He couldn't imagine sporting goods, no matter their variety, as comparable. How could the business exist if he allowed the monumental change his son proposed?

As for Steve, inheritor of his father's creativity, the impasse wasn't pleasant, not because he was rebellious by nature but because his dad often said, "change is good"—a declaration Steve took to heart. Now the third and fourth generations were foundering over this impasse, and generation three seemed immovable. It didn't alleviate the matters of the moment that Fred M—the patriarch that Steve, oldest grandson, got to hunt and fish with, the one who turned the business over to Fred B when Fred returned from the Marine Air Corps—that Fred M died that year at the age of eighty-three.

Fred B wrote of him in the yearly calendar he kept as "the best father a man ever had." Later, when his mother died, Fred wrote about the one who maintained the household where he grew up on $150 a month, as "a truly wonderful mother, demanding, but a strong, strong supporter."

TRAVEL ELSEWHERE

The impasse of father and son provides a providential moment to take a rest from prose, and to sit back as family members often do, with a photo album in their laps, to view the dimensional stability of the past held still. Fred B has written about photography, which he included as part of the essential work of his life, in this way: "Since a child, before ever entering a schoolroom, I have lived for the hunt, the soft shiver of the marsh in the still dark hours of morning, the gold wash of a clear dawn upon the hills, autumn skies in gray and pearl storm, festooned with waterfowl fleeing the summer playgrounds, and always the call of the unseen, over the riverbank, beyond the shore."

He turns to a point citified residents might miss: "Tempered and tuned by eons of hunters, we hardly need hark to hear the call. And in the last one hundred and fifty years, a mere step in the trek of the hunter, man has fashioned a new lance… the camera. What a lance it is! Today's hunt is limited only by the ability of the eye to perceive the quarry solely by our esteem for our fellow man." An explanation of that esteem follows.

He adds in the introduction to his first book of photographs, *A Search to See,* "I was born in Moorhead, Minnesota in 1921 and have lived since within ten miles of my birthplace, except for seven years at college [two at the University of Minnesota in forestry] and in the Marines in World War II. Because of first school, then the war, and then a career in business, my photography had to live until recently upon the time I could extract from those pursuits. Being a hunter, my first photographs were of the wild and wilderness, in still and motion pictures. The beginning of a more thoughtful concern came with attending Ansel Adams' Yosemite Workshop in 1961; there were new standards and hope; the start of collecting the photographs of others, slowly, and the addition of a view camera. The tempo increased and the standards continued to improve into the 1970s, with Leicas, an Olympus, and a 4x5 Graflex, all working around the core of the view camera."

This is the pilot who educated himself on literature and creative writing from four books. He says, "Today, all is subject, from the symphonic rhythms of the metropolis to the remote spits of rock-studded sand where the solitary curlew rests and pipes in vain across a windswept reach. More and more, however, I turn to people, their signs and their tangents, with an endeavor to present them, and their work, *as a matter of form in a spirit of esteem.*" That is, his photographs, particularly the portraits of people, when the viewer seems to be looking at not only a face but into a person's interior, the presentation of this form is a means to esteem the person—a fuller definition of Fred B's earlier statement. He adds, "My search today is for form. Almost any subject can be worthy but only form can make it so.

"Yet for me the work and the increasing perception are as valuable as the final photograph. I can easily translate Thoreau's definition of a philosopher to that of a photographer…not merely to make a few significant photographs, nor even to found a school, but to so love photography as to live according to its dictates a life of simplicity, independence, hard work, and trust. Photography is my well-spring, my expedition, my refuge. Daily I look to it for creation and re-creation."

To narrow the introduction of *A Search To See* to a fervent wish, "My plea would be for you, when looking at my photographs, to become a serious viewer. Your interchange with the photographs can then perhaps be better illustrated if seen as the confrontation of two armies. Within your army, as viewer, each officer and soldier is a unique experience or trait, or prejudice or perception, or learned response, or question, or sympathy or affectation, or any of the almost infinite number of sensitivities in a composite which perceives the photograph, if measured exactly, as few others would. Within the photograph is another composition of visual elements, their organization and presentation determined to a great degree by the photographer who has a different fabric of experience, learnings and traits. The success of the photograph is determined by the number of your different troops it can draw into the visual fray."

This military metaphor echoes the outlook of a Marine fighter pilot who is inviting the viewer with him into a visual fray.

PHOTOGRAPHY
by
FREDERICK B. SCHEEL

Boxelder Grove
Clay County, Minnesota, 1961

New Orleans Waterfront
1957

Gena Veva Garcia Millán La Aduana
Sonora, Mexico, 1982

José Jacinto da Palma
Portugal, 1984

Lodgepoles in the Snow
Idaho, 1976

Julian Alamos
Sonora, Mexico, 1984

Skimmers
Vero Beach, Florida, 1987

Scott Whitney
Fisherman, Owls Head, Maine, 1981

The White Fence
Cape Breton, Nova Scotia, 1980

Sunrise,
Vermillion Lakes, Banff, Canada, c.1951

THE RELATIONSHIP

Now, what do works of art have to do with business? They are the point! If a store can't draw a customer as viewer into the arranged colors and content of a creative matrix, the customer soon feels the affliction of boredom. Any kind of establishment can supply salespeople and floorwalkers peddling product, as it's called, rather than a surrounding atmosphere that creates consumer passion and intensity. Time spent in a store may grow into an artistic experience that edges toward a moment of such inner satisfaction a person will say, as with a problem solved or portrait deciphered, "Ah!"

A customer consumed by the beauty on all sides can only imagine truth and honesty is behind it—how else explain why creative organization resonates with such beauty? Suspended in that revelation the customer is often motivated to purchase whatever is on his or her mind—or not even on the mind, until it appears as if inevitable out of the creative matrix.

The esteemed Russian farmer and educator and writer Leo Tolstoy expressed the concept with perfection in one sentence from his book-length essay *What is Art?* He wrote, "Every work of art results in the one who receives it entering into a certain kind of communion with the one who produced or is producing the art, and with all those who, simultaneously with him, before him, or after him, have received or will receive the same artistic impression."

Steve D realized that customers were spending an average of twenty minutes in a store, time spent only to complete a transaction,

and decided to make SCHEELS an attraction, not a run-of-the-mill store like every other.

In 2007, *Sports Illustrated Kids* chose SCHEELS as the best sporting goods store. "You can buy a baseball glove anywhere," the magazine story stated, "but SCHEELS flagship stores might be the only place where you can buy a baseball glove, ride a Ferris wheel and snack on an ostrich sandwich.

"Stores hold galleries, aquariums, vast atriums with suspended airplanes, restaurants, children's rides, shooting galleries and bowling alleys." The average customer time nowadays in SCHEELS, once Steve's attractive innovations were applied, adds up to more than an hour and a half. How is that measured? "Oh, we have loss prevention in our stores," Steve says. "With loss prevention you can track customers when they come in the front door, you can track them around the store, and if someone looks suspicious you can track them going to the restroom, to the dressing room, and you can track them going out of the store.

"So we found out—wow!—it took me far too long to learn that Cabela's was right! I mean Nordstrom's had a piano player, but Cabela's were the ones I studied and learned that they had aquariums and shooting galleries, because people really enjoyed these things. So when the people in Reno were going to give us a lot of money to build a store, I figure you've got to make it even more an experience, with *two* aquariums and Ferris wheels and shooting galleries and restaurants, and all the rest, and then it was 2008."

People testify how they visit SCHEELS with no plan for a particular purchase—simply to enjoy the ambience, which they do, and end with a purchase anyhow. In addition, the influence of the Internet instills a present-day need, *click-click,* for an interactive shopping experience. If a store can't supply that, the customer will shop at home. Few businesses inspire the kind of confidence customers experience at SCHEELS, and that can be attributed to the creative genius at the heart of the company—a gift with its origins in a father and a gift that never departed from his eight-year-old son.

"One of the biggest things that changed our business," Steve says, "and I don't know now why it took us so long, but if you separate men from women, they'll spend a lot more money and a lot more time. It used to be that all our shoe departments were in one area—men's, women's, youth's were in that area. Now you walk in our stores, women go to the right, men go to the left, and upstairs you have hunting and fishing, and by separating them, women are freer to shop; they spend more money than if their husband's walking right behind them with their credit card, so we're one of the few retail stores in the country to do that, and I don't know if it's something I entirely came up with.

"What I do is, I just sit at my desk—another thing my dad taught me. His office was next to mine, and I remember he walked in one day, and he kind of shut the door rather hard like a Marine Corps Drill Sergeant would do, and he said, 'You know, you're working too hard. You've got to spend more time thinking about the business.' He called it 'Thinking Time,' and now we call it *Think*

Ferris wheel and airplane decorating a lobby of SCHEELS

Time. He said, 'Just put thirty minutes on your calendar every week. Just one thirty-minute period where you close the door, pick out a challenge or opportunity, and figure out how to conquer that.'

"At first it was tough, because I'd look at my calendar and I'd be thinking, *Work.* I should be getting this stuff done, but then it became a half hour twice a week, then it became a half hour every day, and finally became fifty percent of my time, and by 1995 it was simply spend time thinking, 'Hire good people, don't worry about what they're doing; they'll do a great job. Just monitor what they do, and spend time thinking.' That's when I started the study of what to incorporate into the stores.

"Toys R Us in New York City had a Ferris wheel in their Times Square store, now gone, so OK, let's replace that old tree in a store with a Ferris wheel—it moves around! And selling Bavarian nuts that I saw at a Sioux hockey game. Should we try this? Should we sell this fudge I saw at Wisconsin, at Interlocken? I always try fudge after having it at the center of Ginna's Café—named after my mother. This Fuzziwig's Candy concept is probably the best. I saw Fuzziwig's in Vail, so I called them at Durango, and now our stores in Colorado Springs, Johnstown, Eden Prairie, Dallas—and all our future stores will have a large Fuzziwig's Candy Shop." The colorful Fuzziwig's candy line entrances children, and that's another way of drawing the next generation into the SCHEELS experience.

"You know Warren Buffet called us 'The Disneyland of Sporting Goods.' I think that's what it is. Because it's fun to shop at SCHEELS. Dad used to say, 'Have the merchandise the customers want when

A recent addition of newer stores of Fuzziwig's Candy Factory

they want it.' Now I say, 'No, just bring them in, let them enjoy the experience, let them eat in our restaurant, if need be, have coffee, buy candy, shoot in the shooting gallery, ride in the Ferris wheel, if they want, and they'll come back."

FAMILY CHANGE

Stocking as a youngster, serving as employee and then president and CEO, Steve D says, "I did everything from delivery to paint mixing to cake decoration in the older stores. I taught a class on Wilton cake decorating as part of the management training program years ago. I started full time in 1972 after time in the Army."

In the midst of this busy life, the first son of Steve D arrived; he received the encouraging creative name of Steve Michael, and was born, his father says, "On January 15, 1971, in the U.S. Army at a cost of $8.80 at Fort Carson, Colorado. One of my best friends, a high school friend, Michael Triegs, still a good friend, lives in Des Moines, Iowa, so now Steve *Michael*.

"He has three children. His oldest son, Branden, just got married. Branden is twenty-seven and works in our stores. He's a world-class Iron Man who races all over the world, but his racing schedule is coming down, and he works full-time for us now—just got into the assistant-store-leader program in our Colorado store in Johnstown.

"Steve Michael's middle son, Hunter, is completely differently wired from Branden. He's into computers and does coding full-time for Scheels Information Systems, or SIS. And Steve Michael's daughter, Miranda, is in a curling tournament right now in Williston. She's a senior in high school and works part-time, filling online orders for us in Fargo.

"Steve Michael is the oldest, and the next son born to Sandee and me is Brandon. He's a store leader in Mankato. He's a real people person. Steve Michael got the gift of a high IQ, and inherited some of the traits of his grandpa. Brandon runs our Mankato store. Our daughter Stacy lives in Detroit Lakes. My adopted daughter, Christy, is married to Byron Snider, the head of our IT department in town, Scheels Information Systems. The other adopted daughter—I consider both mine—Susanne, lives in New York City. Her husband is a licensed architect.

"Susanne is in film casting. She went to Boston University and graduated top of her class in film and communications. She does casting both on her own and for Coen Brothers films. I don't know if you saw the movie *The Blind Side* with Sandra Bullock about a black football player, the state of Mississippi? It was a great movie and I watch it all the time to stay and see the credit for casting: *Susanne Scheel*. She's doing well and has two young kids in New York. We're flying out there for two days of Christmas."

S teve Michael has risen through the ranks of SCHEELS in the manner of his father, never expecting a favor nor requesting one. The other children have done well in the family company, now the seventh generation, and some have taken an independent route in life itself, as Steve D did in the 1990s. About that turning point he says, "My wife Sandee and I got along well. We just parted ways. It was that simple, and it was good for Sandee. I think she's really enjoying life, as I am, too. I adopted Eileen's two girls after we married in 1997, on one of the coldest winters in history, twenty-five below that January day. Shortly after that the two girls approached me and said they didn't want me to be their step-dad; they wanted me to be their dad.

"I said, 'That's fine, but you have to wait six months, because that's quite a step. You've got a biological dad, too, and he has his challenges, but he's still your dad.' Six months to the day, they were back in my office at home and cornered me and said, 'We still want this to happen.' So we arranged for the adoption of them, and in court—I knew the judge at the time—the judge called the girls up front because it was just our attorney, my wife and me, and he said to them, 'I know your dad is an upstanding citizen. How about the two of you?' He scared the bejesus out of them.

"But no, no real problems, the kids get along pretty well. The Warfords are our friends—John the mayor of Bismarck for twelve years—and they were at the wedding."

TO THEN

About his early career, Steve D says, "I was an assistant manager in Fargo in 1973 to 1974, and then managed that store for the next two years." It was at this time that a touching four-generation photograph of the Scheel family was taken, with Fred B far left, Fred M next, with a blond-haired boy, head down, standing in his lap, who seems to be saying "No more pictures!" and Steve D far right.

Steve says of the time, "I closed our last farm store in Casselton, North Dakota, in 1976, and sold the building. I opened Sioux Falls in May 1977 with Deb Friman as my assistant manager. They don't get any better than Deb. Now, when we open a new store, we send

Four Generations: Fred B, far left, Fred M with Steve M in his lap, and Steve D

about fifty people full-time to that store. They stay as part of the team and grow from there. When I went to Sioux Falls, I was construction manager, general manager, I was bookkeeper, I did the hiring—everything. There were no assistant managers or line leaders or buyers to help. That is simply the way we did it, without help or computers! I had a hiring office in our small house where we lived, and applicants came to interview and apply.

"Deb Friman said she'd like to move to Sioux Falls, so she and her husband Mike came with me, and Mike worked for Pam Oil. Deb was the only experienced worker we had. She was the merchandising manager and made sure the floor looked good. She did a tremendous job!

"After I left Sioux Falls, she decided to go to Nike, but then came back and worked for us until she retired. She was an absolute gem— one of the hardest workers I've known in my life. I wish she would have stayed with us longer so I could have written her a bigger ESOP check when she retired."

Steve is naming the Employee Stock Ownership Plan, yet another innovation of his, backed by his father, and installed at SCHEELS.

LARGER FAMILY

"So… I managed Sioux Falls from 1977 to 1980, then Moorhead 1980 to 1986 and Southside Fargo from 1987 to 1989. I was line leader, the buyer for archery, baseball, hunting, guns, camping, hockey, skates, hunting clothing and footwear, inline skates, sporting games, fishing, bikes, and bike accessories between 1978 and 1988. I became President, CEO, and board chairman in 1990, after thirteen years on the executive committee."

Jan Hook, the manager who hired Mike Welu at Cedar Falls, headed-up several SCHEELS stores, and in 1990 was elected to the SCHEELS executive committee. "It was not only a highlight in my career it was one of the single greatest opportunities of my life," he says. "By joining the committee I was able to help set policy for where we wanted the company to go. The advantage we had was a culture that was passed on to us. I believe all of the decisions we made when I sat on the board were based on that culture: Customer first, and: Our people are our greatest asset. The board meetings were never boring. It seemed that nearly every decision had some form of heated debate. Many times there would be more than one red face at the table. But when the debate was done and the vote was finalized, we knew we were united. Literally, hundreds of the best moments of my life happened in that board room."

Steve D extends a special note of gratitude to board members and former managers who worked to create SCHEELS present-day standing: "Bob Scheel worked with Robert Alin in reviving the Southside Fargo Scheels Hardware. It was about to close when a considerable number of pleas to keep it open were raised by south residents once they learned of the situation. The reason for closing was the construction of a new 60,000 square-foot SCHEELS All Sports Store on 13th Avenue South in Fargo.

"On October 1, 1974, all the partnerships were converted into one corporation with Charles as president. The number and the size of stores continued to grow with the transition to fully sports stores. I was really close with Bob and not very close with Charles. Bob was fourteen years older, and I just gave the eulogy at his funeral. Bob didn't like the sporting goods business. He loved the lawn and garden and hardware business. When the Southside Fargo store went to sports, he said it was time to bail, so I went to Fargo and took over. He had opened the first store in Bismarck, in the Arrowhead Plaza, and then moved back to Fargo and opened the Southside Fargo Hardware Store.

"It's still hardware, the Home and Hardware Store, and he and my mentor, Bob Alin, brought in the current manager, Mark Hulbert, who is the son of our former president, Steve Hulbert. Now Mark is retiring on January first, so it's another progression. I learned the numbers from Lloyd Paulson, and disciplined organization from Dad, and I learned people skills from Bob Alin. He was probably the best people person in Fargo.

"People would come into the store, and I'd say, 'Can I help you?' and hear 'No, I'm waiting for Bob. Got to talk to him about life insurance.' We're in a hardware store! 'Can I talk to Bob about what doctor I need?' Well, that was kind of our history to that point, and I was privileged to work with incredible people who influenced me and gave me a foundation for what I've done at SCHEELS over the last fifty years. Dad was the person who drove the wagon train and he was a good driver. He whipped up high expectations, high standards. I expect he expected a lot of all of us. I know that. All the store managers and leaders know that.

"Dad always said, 'If you have the merchandise the customers want, when they want it, without excess, you're in good shape. That's the tough part of the retail business; what they want, when they want it, without excess. The biggest problem most retailers have is they end up with inventory at the end of the year, and bankers don't want to be paid with inventory. They want cash. It's a struggle to achieve that fine

line, but Dad taught us well: keep eight weeks of merchandise in stock, track your records. We used to keep them manually, now we track them digitally and try to keep eight weeks of merchandise in stock—and if a little tougher to get, maybe twelve weeks. But ideally, it's eight weeks supply of the merchandise the customer wants.

"I was happy to work under Bob Alin," Steve says. His reasoning is that from Bob Alin he learned, above all, the need to sharpen his outlook on every person he met, from associates on the floor to whatever customer he might encounter in whatever situation. It was this open attitude to others that enabled him to see the power of removing the final wall of retail and immersing customers in an artistic ambience of the kind he started to create in each store. This attitude, rather than a sales pitch, was a true innovation.

"But it's the inventory that's necessary to run a business," Steve adds, "and that's true down to this day. Of course, when we're tracking over two-million SKUs a year now in the business—Stock-Keeping Unit, alphanumeric codes assigned to each product—and we move to five seasons, from spring to summer to fall to winter to holiday, it gets more complex. But I think we have the best system in retail. I'd put it up against Walmart or anyone else."

EARLIER TRIALS

Mike Welu, who became an early store manager, said, "I applied for a job with Scheels at the Waterloo store and the manager didn't hire me. He did tell me a new store manager was at the Cedar Falls and might be hiring. So I went to meet Jan Hook. At the end of my second interview with Hook he told me I "lacked a salesperson aura." But if I wanted to try to earn a job, I could come to the store that weekend and work Saturday and Sunday. If I sold over $1,000 each day, he would hire me.

"I showed up on Saturday morning and Hook gave me a yellow shirt and said good luck. Zero training. He didn't even introduce me to the other salespeople, who weren't pleased to be competing with me. It was early January, and selling $1,000 a day at Cedar Falls in January was nearly hopeless, though I didn't know that. I sold a lot of Columbia coats. I also remember selling a gun, without any idea how to complete the paperwork. Somebody completed it for me. I surpassed the $1,000 in sales and returned on Sunday and did it again. Hook offered me a job, but said I couldn't start until February, because he didn't have me in his salary budget for January.

"And that is how I started at Scheels.

"The store at Cedar Falls was half hardware and half sporting goods. I sold lawnmowers, fertilizer, tools, and even a hot water heater. We had only one in stock at the time, so it wasn't a difficult sale. The hottest product on the sales floor was the Schwinn Air Dyne Exercise Bike. They sold for $700 each, and on a good day you could sell two or three. I don't know how many Air Dynes the company sold, but I have to believe the profit off the Air Dyne was a large percentage of their corporate profit for a few years.

Fred B in the years he was writing poetry

"My first meeting with FBS [Fred B Scheel] was shortly after I became assistant manager at Cedar Falls. Fred was present for a store visit, and he was in the shoe area. I walked up to him and stuck out my hand for a shake and said, 'Mr. Scheel, I'm Mike Welu.' He shook my hand and said, 'What can I do for you?' I said I just wanted to introduce myself. He said, 'Well, you have done that.' And turned and walked away." Not a people person.

"The first store of my own was Billings on 24th street. It was an older store in terrible condition. Fixtures were old and built poorly. Somebody had the idea to paint the entire back wall in pastel colors. Every four feet was a different shade of pink, yellow, or baby blue. In addition, the store was dirty. One of the worst areas was the basement. It appeared nobody had thrown out any old fixture or display for twenty years. There was barely an aisle to walk through the basement.

"I hired a new cleaning service and gave them strict protocols. And I cleaned out the basement myself. Since I had no money in my budget for extra hours, I would work in my shirt and tie all day, then switch to jeans and a T-shirt for an evening of hauling junk out of the basement. I filled a forty foot container of trash. I believe that cleaning the basement was one of the actions that gave FBS a favorable impression of me.

"He came to visit quite often that year, at least three times, maybe four. They were unannounced visits, but Scheels managers had a network that kept me informed of his whereabouts. He would arrive with a list of what he wanted to see. It made a guy sweat a little, but it was effective in making sure we did things correctly. What I dreaded most about FBS' visits was he always wanted to go to a local restaurant to eat, and I was expected to drive. Usually my truck was full of dirt and dog hair. My dog always rode in the front seat. If I suspected FBS was due, I cleaned my truck well, and didn't allow my dog into it until after he left. I passed muster every visit."

Steve Scheel adds, "In the 60's and 70's when dad or the store supervisor would visit, they used yellow pads and carbon paper to leave the notes for the store manager. The advent of the copy machine made life far easier, and soon to follow were fax machines. After a trial to make sure it worked between two stores all the stores bought fax machines."

TO NOW

In December of 2021, in the relocated and partially finished office of Steve D—with photographs and portraits and publications stacked on tables and desks—a huge digital display on the wall tracks every purchase that takes place at each store location. A huge set of crimson numerals in the upper left of the display keeps a running record of the sales, its numbers constantly tumbling. This is the end point of the best tracking system in retail, the one Steve said he would put up against Walmart and others.

"It's all built in-house," he says to the visitors interested in the history of the Scheel family past as it relates to present-day SCHEELS business. "We have our own coders, our own programmers, and we do it all in-house. This is the Scheel Information Service. With it we can track all the inventory we keep in the stores for eight weeks or so, in a pretty involved process. Every cash register in every store is connected to that store's computer, and those feed into our main computer over at the new corporate office building."

Steve points out that the electronic board is updated every three minutes to impress on his visitors the speed this innovation has in its effects on the entire SCHEELS retail network. The visitors watch the numbers fed from thirty stores continue to tumble past multiple figures in an hour. More than a dozen headings of specific inventories cover the rest of the board, such as women's shoes, ammunition, skis—you name it—tumbling with every single specific sale, with an arrow at the side of each that points up or down. These indicate its rise or fall over a period of previous sales.

"Now it's high-margin shops," Steve says. "A month ago, it was ammunition and shotguns, low-margin shops, now it's all athletic clothes, which is line 38, women's athletics, line 39. They're all high-margin shops, which makes me smile even more," he adds, as he studies the display.

"There at the top is the number-one shop for the day—of the ninety-nine or so shops that we track—and down from it are the top twenty others. It tells you where people are buying merchandise right now." So even the particular stores are kept track of, and he points out a set of staggered line graphs at the top of the display: the red line represents sales of last year, the yellow line yesterday's sales, and the conclusion, as Steve points out, is that the sales of the moment are exceeding both last year and yesterday over every hour—an innovative addition of his business philosophy: keeping track of every retail sale up to the minute, rather than figuring it out later.

— Steve D at his desk, a portrait of his grandfather at his shoulder

He doesn't credit this entirely to his efforts, and each situation has its personal, everyday implications. "Our vendors, our buyers worked so hard this year that we're one of the few retailers with the merchandise that we want to sell in place. Everybody else was working their forty hours a week while our people were working eighty hours a week, and we have the merchandise right now. Fleet Farm, Walmart, a lot of others, have empty shelves, even grocery stores do. My wife wants a certain kind of saltine cracker. She sends me a text, so I stop at the grocery store on the way home, call, 'Honey, they don't have it.' Don't get 'em. Makes my life easy."

DIGITAL READOUT

The visitors find intriguing the way Steve as CEO saw that the entire electronic system was built on his business model: speedy implementation of inventory and sales through innovation established by the company itself. In 1987 he hired IBM, he says, to move SCHEELS into the computer age. "They wanted the tail to wag the dog, and we said, 'No, no. We've got the best manual system in retail. We want you to mirror our manual system that we call our Basic Stock Inventory.' We had stock inventory for every vendor we carried. So we fired IBM and hired our own programmers and built our own system internally."

"What's amazing to me is our people on the floor now can walk through with their—I think it's TC52s and go like this"—a sweep of his hand—"and tell you what stores stock the product, which one has it now, how many they have, and how long that inventory should last."

A visitor hurries to say, "The scanner system you have now is tremendous! It's fast. I was in your Bismarck store looking for boots for my boys, and I said, 'Do you have this in size eight?' And the guy went *beep*—'No, but we have it in Fargo. We can have it here for you tomorrow.' I said, 'OK! I mean it was a snap of a finger, done. No headache!'"

An elderly visitor regrets SCHEELS could not fill an online order for "base layer wool," which used to be called long underwear, but was informed it would be necessary for him to go to a store to pick it up—"So they can tell me it itches?" he asks.

Steve would not let an opportunity pass to engage this customer in inspired service, considering his love for retail, and he led the older man to understand that the newer, base-layer industry was more complex, and that he, Steve, for instance, preferred Under Armor, because "Under Armor makes a top or bottom of 2.0, 3.0, and 4.0. They call the 4.0 their 'North of Ninety,' meaning Interstate 90. I've found 4.0 is better than wool, and 2.0 will do if it's not too cold. But if I'm going out at fifteen or twenty below to blow snow from my driveway, I put on 4.0, top and bottom."

This led to a discussion of outdoor winter exertions, widespread in the Scheel family, and the older fellow suggested SCHEELS should install a chainsaw booth. "I've got a big Stihl," Steve said, the chain saw preferred by most professional woodcutters, "and I've got the hand-held battery-operated Stihl. We had an oak tree that needed

A sleek display of bicycles and their pictured potential terrain

SIOUX FALLS

Many of Steve's undertakings turn out well, except for the impasse with his father over selling only sporting goods in a new store. That store was the first Sioux Falls, South Dakota, store he was given to open and oversee in 1977, which means he and his family moved there. He says, "The store was only 10,717 square feet"—compared to present stores of several hundred thousand—"but we got it all in there. We had a motor shop. We had a bike shop. We had it all. Then by 1980, they chose me to come back and run the Moorhead store, our biggest store at the time, and to *supervise* Sioux Falls.

"A young man called Tim Gette was going down to take over for me, so I said, 'Tim, I'm supervisor of the store now, and we can make that store all sporting goods.' He said, 'We can?' I said, 'We can, just don't screw it up. Just don't tell Dad.'

"Of course Dad found out, right?—because I had to request from our ad manager—I had to request ads for going-out-of-business sales on hardware and houseware and lawn and garden. But Dad, well, he let it go, and it went really well, and the next year hardware was going out of St. Cloud, Minnesota, Mankato, Minnesota, and Waterloo, Iowa, and they were becoming all-sports stores"—suggesting that Steve's latest innovation was the first step in the entire transformation of SCHEELS as a retail business.

"The margin was quite a bit higher, but the sales gain, where we were having five to six percent sales gain in our hardware stores, we were having twenty-five to thirty percent gain in the sporting goods

to come down at the lakes two summers ago, so I told the guy who came to cut it down, 'Take it off at ten feet, because I'm going to carve a pelican sculpture in there.' Sculpture was the only class at St. Olaf I got an A+ in, so I figured, I can do this. I bought three different blades. The last one was real sharp points, and I carved the feathers and details with it. It turned out fairly well, my first ever."

stores." The gain in income was enough to persuade any perceptive businessperson, such as his father, and Steve adds, "It was also a lot more fun, because when people come in to buy a water heater that's rusted out or a lawn mower because the old one doesn't work anymore, instead of buying water skis or a rifle or a new coat, they're going out in an entirely different mood. Instead of, 'Damn thing broke again…,' they're happy with the new!

"When I left Sioux Falls with our family in 1980, we came from a progressive school system, and we interviewed with several schools in Fargo, West Fargo, and Moorhead, and found Moorhead the best. It's one town with one school system, basically one school, and everybody's a Moorhead "Spud." We enjoy it. It's where I coached hockey."

NEW REALMS

About the SCHEELS present administration, to bring matters up to date after the advent of his creative innovations, Steve says, "Our current president is Todd Anderson, who came from our Billings store. My son Steve Michael is CEO. Our president runs the day-to-day operations, with help from a lot of other supervisors. Steve Michael as CEO watches the financials with our CFO, Michelle Killeran. He provides a kind of vision of where we're going to go, and meets with developers and is also involved in supervising eight of our biggest stores.

"All officers are elected, and then re-elected on an annual basis—they are recommended by the executive committee and voted on by all our partners in the business, our retired managers, our current store leaders. We have probably one-hundred-fifty partners in the business now who have bought SCHEELS stock. They're also all given the advisement of the executive committee. We're open in all we do. They get reports on all we do. We're a wide-open company."

In the period of the eighties into the nineties Steve's dad worked on poems he had begun in the fifties. Steve's new leadership role at SCHEELS freed Fred B to turn to the art he had neglected the longest. He records his detailed methods of composition in the introduction to *Poetry and Other Writings*: "During the 1950s I started writing a few poems, most of which I did not finish until I picked them up some thirty years later.

"At that time, our involvement in civic work and our growing children eased enough to afford more time for photography, as well as travel and acrobatic flying, and a resumption of writing. My brothers retired to other interests about 1990, and son, Steve, was elected by the leadership to lead the business, now sporting goods. I maintain an active, but much reduced, role in our business, and began a growing thrust in our church through the development of mission work.

"In the 1980s and '90s, upon the resumption of writing, I completed or revised those works begun thirty years earlier.

"I write with about twenty pieces in a group, building and revising them in rotation, working each through perhaps twenty to a hundred visits over a period of a few months to two to three years. When an idea arises, I add it to the group, and when one seems completed or grows uninteresting, I remove it for typing or discard.

"My writing goal each week varies from about eight to fifteen hours with an average near twelve. Such time includes writing poetry, personal letters, an occasional essay and, but rarely, a story. Other than letters it is purely for enjoyment, and to see if perhaps I may have a touch of talent from whence, with practice, cometh a modest skill.

"Beauty or truth inspires in the turn of a few words, as in Poe's 'And the silken, sad, uncertain rustling of each purple curtain thrilled me,' or Melville's 'The warmly cool, clear ringing, perfumed, overflowing redundant days were like crystal goblets of Persian sherbet, heaped up, flaked up with rose water snow,' or each and every line of Kipling's 'If.' A series of sensitive visions or strikingly phrased observations or eternal truths rises from the page."

Fred B exercised further family generosity in 2007, when he donated over six hundred photographic prints he had collected from nineteenth and twentieth century photographic artists to the Minneapolis Institute of Art. Colleen Sheehy, a director of the Plains Art Museum in Fargo, where an earlier mounting and exhibition of Fred B's work had taken place, said about the exhibition, "Fred saw pattern and form—a sense of order—in the world. He helps us see the beauty all around us."

That is the essence of the creative gift; it opens avenues of perception to the central beauty of creation, an ordering of every detail into its design. It's that perception that allowed Steve D to see through the persiflage of retail business into the heart of matters: reinventing business into an orderly design while maintaining the creative essence of keeping abreast. As a cyclist he took part in semi-professional races, not with anyone as prominent as Lance Armstrong but with the mayor of the capital city, Bismarck, a U.S. record holder in the high hurdles, a true competitor who was not as hard-nosed as Steve, Steve says, and the competition taught him that he could not lag if he wanted to attain the goals he could initially only sense.

The expenditure of athletic energy continues to exhilarate Steve. As for bicycles, he assembled and repaired and ordered racing accessories for all sorts and models up to Trek over the years, and let it be known in a general sense, in a talk he gave at the University of Mary's Lunch and Learn series, sponsored by the Gary Tharaldson School of Business and the Bismarck-Mandan Chamber of Commerce, that in any comparison to hardware one might make, "sporting goods are more fun."

POET PROTEST

His father Fred considered sporting goods a luxury—after his time with cameras and a stunt plane, one might wonder? Yes, a luxury, and received Steve's first suggested change to the business of Scheels as too high a risk. The original model had worked too well for eighty years in the agricultural area where most stores were located. So Steve had to become a negotiator and persuade his dad to allow him to stock a *larger* selection of sporting goods at Sioux Falls. He was allowed that, and the increased stock sold well.

Scheels creating sports superstore

13th Avenue Best store to become firm's new home

By Jonathan Knutson
The Forum

Fargo-based Scheels plans to open a flagship "sports superstore" along Fargo's 13th Avenue in the building currently occupied by the Best store. Best announced last week that it's vacating the building.

Scheels will have 45,000 square feet of retail space and a sports repair and service facility at its new site, as well as another 30,000 square feet for offices and warehouse.

The new store, to be known as Scheels All Sports, also will house the company's corporate office, advertising office and corporate clothing buying office, all currently scattered throughout Fargo-Moorhead.

Renovation is expected to begin by Feb. 1, with the store scheduled to open in July.

"This new store will be large enough for us to offer Scheels customers a collection of full-service sports specialty shops under one roof," said Steve Hulbert, Scheels

Hulbert   Steve Scheel

executive vice president and manager of the new store.

Demand for sporting goods is growing rapidly, and Scheels wants to accommodate it.

"We need a lot more space for sports," Hulbert said.

Scheels will close its store at 1417 S. University Drive, Fargo. Employees of the University Drive store will be offered positions at the new store or the other Scheels stores in Fargo-Moorhead, Hulbert said.

The new store will employ about 125 people.

Scheels owns its University Drive

An artist's rendering of the new Scheels superstore on 13th Avenue in Fargo.

building and plans to sell it, he said.

Although the company considered several potential sites for the new store, he said, the Best location was its first choice.

Remodeling will cost an estimated $750,000 to $1 million.

The company was founded by Frederick A. Scheel in 1902 in Sabin, Minn.

His son, Frederick M. Scheel, became owner of the business in 1919. Fred B. Scheel, Charles P. Scheel and Robert Scheel, grandsons of Frederick A. Scheel, joined

the company in 1946, 1947 and 1964, respectively.

Steve Scheel, son of Fred B. Scheel, was named president in 1989 after managing stores in Fargo, Moorhead and Sioux Falls, S.D.

■ See **SCHEELS**, Page B6

Notice of Scheels All Sports opening in Fargo, with a new logo

He has said that when he went next door to his dad's office with an idea and said, "What do you think?" his dad said, "What do *you* think?" and a mystery too elusive for language to contain may have occurred in that exchange. Steve was facing the greatest creative consciousness for miles, the one who not only produced artistic photographs and poetry and prose but conceived acrobatic programs in the air—one who wanted viewers of his work to enter a creative fray— this encompassing consciousness contained so many possibilities that when his son stated an idea that idea became incarnate in Fred B, and he carried it to fruition by saying, "Just do it." *Enact the thought I'm able to see now that you've named it*, as he may have explained once the spark of creation dimmed.

Why otherwise would Fred B, the third generation to conform to a pattern, send his fist in a slam to his desk, and why, when he learned of the clandestine fall from grace of his son, would he not confront or scold Steve? The details remain sealed between the two, but Fred seems to have agreed to the move and was willing for other stores to follow his son's model. The source of creative power that energized and enlivened Fred B he now saw blossom not in external displays, such as poetry or the lyric prose of book introductions or photography or aerial acrobatics, but inside the very heart of the business itself, in the hands of his companionable son.

Steve says, "His concern I think was, back in the day, that sports was something you kind of did as a sidelight and weren't too serious about. He knew people who hunted seriously and fished seriously but few who played hockey and football in college, like I did. Sports weren't like they are today—sports is now a lifestyle, and I think we hit it right at just the right time."

SCHEELS first new all-sports superstore opened in Grand Forks in 1989, at 30,000 square feet, and the move to sporting goods seemed news of the day, considering an article by Johnathan Knutson in a 1994 *Fargo Forum*: "Fargo-based Scheels plans to open a flagship 'sports superstore' along Fargo's 13th Avenue in the building currently occupied by the Best store. Best announced last week that it's vacating the building.

"The new store will have 45,000 square feet of retail space and a sports repair and service facility at its new site, as well as another 30,000 square feet for offices and warehouse.

"The new store, to be known as Scheels All Sports will also house the company's corporate office, advertising office and corporate clothing buying office, all currently scattered throughout Fargo-Moorhead…

"'This new store will be large enough for us to offer Scheels customers a collection of full-service sports specialty shops under one roof,' said Steve Hulbert, Scheels executive vice president and manager of the new store…

"'We need a lot more space for sports,' Hulbert said.

"Scheels will close its store at 1417 S. University Drive, Fargo. Employees of the University Drive store will be offered positions at the new store or the other Scheels stores in Fargo-Moorhead, Hulbert said.

"The new store will employ about 125 people."

GENERATIONAL ARTISTRY

It's a scientific mystery to explain how a particular person in a family takes on aspects of the family's history, from its origins to its religion to generational qualities, including clarity of thought and purpose and an unshakable desire to do well in an adopted country, by means of one or more creative arts—in other words, everything so far mentioned about the Scheel family. It's a mystery to explain how that accumulated heritage one day appears, whether by bloodline or genetic makeup or providence or the act of God himself—nobody can say with certainty how or why—but it happens in families of both high and low degree: *the atavistic appearance of the characteristics of an ancestor.*

This is a transfer or appearance of talents referred to in more than one book by a cadet pilot in the British Royal Air Force who trained in Canada during WWI, and later piloted his Waco cabin aircraft to New Orleans to gather material for *Pylon,* a novel about racing and barnstorming pilots, the Nobel-prize-winning American author, William Faulkner. A look into the character of Steve Scheel at the age of eight seems captured in research from the 1990s. In *Breakpoint and Beyond: Mastering the Future Today* published in 1992, George Land and Beth Jarman cited a study that few have heard of and fewer understand: 1,600 children, from the ages of three to five, were tested for creativity, and it was discovered that at the age of five, ninety percent of those tested scored in the realm of creative genius.

When the same group of 1,600 was tested at the age of ten, it was discovered that thirty percent scored in the area of creative genius. Once more, at the age of fifteen, the same group underwent testing, and only ten percent scored near the level of creative genius. A sadder, conclusive statistic was established when results were gathered on 280,000 adults and it was discovered that only two percent reached the level of creative genius.

The result of the testing was that *non-creative behavior is learned.*

Creativity not only fades but travels down an unreachable cave of the unconscious as young people are told or taught that the opinions and evaluations and beliefs of others are of greater importance than their own. Maintaining or striving for the original creative gift is a valid response to the teaching of Jesus, who says that those who wish to learn from him must become as children. Nicholas Black Elk states the paradox in a similar way: "Grown men may learn from very little children, for the hearts of little children are pure, and, therefore, the Great Spirit may show to them many things older people miss." Only in an unquestioning, unadulterated state can one rest in the infinite creativity of Christ, where a centrally important lesson lodges: truth is beauty. The compilation of both truth and beauty is holiness. God exists in the beauties of His holiness.

Few are able to think according to the creative distinction of God, who says his Word is truth—the way that sets adherents free—and the invitation of Jesus to become as a child means one should focus on the creative genius of God-made-man, ultimately infinite, in whatever gifts a person might have been given. When the exercise of a given gift takes place in the framework of the freeing nature of truth, the result is beauty comparable to divine creation. Lift your eyes to nature's surround!

This is the surround that hunter and photographer evaluate in minute detail, and that the executive vice president of Hartford Accident and Indemnity Insurance and Pulitzer Prize-winning poet Wallace Stevens meant when he said, "The most beautiful thing in the world is, of course, the world itself." A central concern of Stevens, as with Scheel generation three and four, was the transformative power of the imagination.

In such a context, *What is work?* Work is commonly defined as the expenditure of energy for a purpose, but if energy is carried out in a surround of beauty, and a person enjoys expending energy as competitors in sports do, it can be said that the expenditure of energy can lead to calm at the center of beauty, within the nature of the Creator of life.

Never since the age of eight did Steve D view what he did as work. It appears he was experiencing the joy hidden from the wise and prudent, according to St. Paul the Apostle, and revealed to infants and babes. One question rises from the joy that work inspires—can joy increase in its levels?

With further creative innovation when the potential for it occurs, yes, as the opportunity for interior innovations occurs in new stores in new states for Steve Scheel, as will happen three times in 2023-24 (see map on page 93), along with stores moving to improved state locations. The creative remastering of the sporting goods industry is the reason for SCHEELS phenomenal financial ascent.

ECCE HOMO

Steve D does not present a remarkable front to those who encounter him in the Fargo store, where he spends his time in recent years, as in attending to his recent visitors. He likes to walk the floor and meet people; likes to hear their responses to merchandise displays and the store itself. He's not a flashy dresser or prima donna who expects the sea to part when he appears in one of the many SCHEELS stores. He's trim and athletic, as Scheels have been—not a single photo of even one of them appearing overweight. He's a cyclist and game-bird hunter, neither nondescript nor flamboyant in dress. He radiates buoyant childlike pleasure, is positive, often smiles—smile creases extending from his eyes and creasing both sides of his mouth, suggesting the smile is central to his personality.

An observer notes, "He is soft spoken but a forceful presence. He makes a point of being friendly with staff and treating mistakes as learning opportunities." You probably walked right past him on a visit to SCHEELS, and he was sure to notice you. He pays attention to the reaction of customers in the aisles and on the floors of SCHEELS.

"My favorite part of the job is walking out on the floor," he says, "and meeting customers and our people face-to-face, and I'll have two boards of digital displays in my office in another week. The one board you see, but the next board tells me, right as I sit here, who the leaders are every single day; which shops are leading out of the ninety-nine we track; who are the people who lead in sales in those shops, and which cashiers are voted the best. That's a favorite, being on the floor, keeping up, but it's writing checks to ESOP employees, or writing a note with the check—that's most enjoyable!"

Steve entered the family business at such an early age that when he was asked after he was elected president what his favorite task was, he said he never considered he was faced with any "tasks" at work. For further clarity he added, "I have never come to work a day in my life, because I thoroughly enjoy what I do and those who surround me in this business."

He seems to mean not only associates present in the store each day, but the effect of inherited generations, because he goes on to say, "I enjoy looking at the past to see just how far we have come, and I enjoy planning for our future and working on new locations. The great people all around me have built our company into something in which I take a great deal of pride."

He enjoys the time he is able to spend with his grandchildren, he says, perhaps recalling his father's absence at similar events, and adds, "My wife and I enjoy skiing, kayaking, biking, hiking, and snowshoeing. My English setters and I enjoy pheasant hunting, and I archery hunt in the fall."

DAD'S SIDE

The font of creative genius was not fixed. Fred B recognized his son's creative powers partly as an inheritance, and Steve's imagination was only beginning to be released. For Fred B, a pastime had to be curtailed, and on a sad day for him, he wrote, "Came 1997, after twenty-two years of acrobatic, flying, I sold my exquisite little Pitts acrobatic plane to reduce exposure and concentrate on other interests which might better use that time."

As Steve has said, "Too many of his friends were being killed." The accidents of acrobatic planes are horrific, as viewed in videos, especially when performing inverted flat spins too close to earth, apparently seeing themselves elsewhere, with only an altimeter and virtual horizon. The pilots are flying by the seat of their pants in the truest sense—"No instruments!" Steve claims—often in an open cockpit, and can lose their sense of the horizon or up and down and "auger it in," as pilots put it in graphic terms.

The idea of all-sporting-goods stores was only the first of five creative adaptations Steve D added to open wide the family business. These five elements would define SCHEELS as one of the innovative retail entities of the century. Number one, the switch, of course, from hardware to sporting goods; two, the concept of each store as an aesthetic experience; three, leadership training that Steve instituted, with added SCHEELS University training on the knowledge of products; four, working with his father Fred B to establish an Employee Stock Ownership Plan (ESOP), so everybody in every store would be working toward the same goal; and five, his pushing the advanced use of computer technology, so that on the far wall of his office, facing the desk where he sits, the digital display of sales at every location is updated minute by minute.

Steve D at a favorite product to assemble, sell, and ride in his racing endeavors

Every one of these innovations, as creative as the external works of creation of his father, Fred B, in literary and photographic realms, were installed instead at the heart of the family business.

Steve D says, "There is no way I did it by myself. I had a lot of help. I am surrounded by incredible people, and I walk around in awe of them every day. I had these visions, but you've got to have people you bump projects off of and thoughts off of, and most of the time I got a thumbs up. They would pick up ideas I mentioned and carry them farther than I thought. They developed a passion for the business and took it to new heights. And it helped that my dad was always saying, 'If you think it's the right thing to do, just do it.'"

The new SCHEELS stores were called the "Disneyland of Sporting Goods Stores," by Warren Buffet. Buffet's interest grew when he noted the increasing addition of stores with sumptuous, enveloping interiors. And the SCHEELS stores were being built each one larger than the last to accommodate the growing range of sporting goods— from hunting to camping to golfing to skiing and the rest, along with each sport's clothing and footwear.

In 1989, as the family business was being altered with increased technology, Steve M, Steve D's oldest son, began working at the Southside Scheels Hardware in Fargo, which would remain a hardware store, and what was it he did? He was a part-time stocker of shelves, as his father had been. He says, "That lasted about two weeks before I was selling shoes, and soon after I was selling water skis and bikes. I began as an assistant sales leader in 1995, and my first store as manager was the Moorhead store in 1998."

EARLIER VIEW

An article by Andrea Gleiter in a University of Mary publication of 2017, *360 Review*, contains a section titled *Bigger, Biggest, & Almost Bust*. "When the first SCHEELS in Grand Forks opened in 1989 at 30,000 square feet, it was the company's largest venue so far," she wrote. For clarity Steve adds, "We did not build a store from 1980 to 1989, because of interest rates and inflation. If I were to sign a lease and open in Grand Forks, I wondered, *Could we afford it?* If we bought wrong in ten percent of our inventory—where our cash is tied up—and we're borrowing at thirteen to fourteen-and-a-half percent— we could not be long by ten percent of our inventory. Bankers do not want to be paid with excess inventory.

"I remember Chuck Scheel calling me on one of those years like '86 or '87, and saying 'Can you send another $10,000 from your Southside Store? We need it to pay off these loans!' Interest rates were so high it was a struggle. And when at last they started coming down, we built Grand Forks, and of course now interest rates have been so low for so long, that our young people—they've never faced a serious challenge. They weren't there in 2007-2008, which was the last serious challenge we faced."

As it turned out, it became clear with the Grand Forks store that additional space was going to be needed down the line, and the next store opened in Eau Claire, Wisconsin, in 1995, at 50,000 square feet. Steve saw that within six months it was too small.

A pontoon plane adds the dimension of "Outfitter" to SCHEELS ·

"A year later, the Fargo SCHEELS opened at 60,000 square feet," Gleiter wrote. "Then in 1998, a new SCHEELS opened near Iowa City, Iowa, this time with two stories, which doubled the location's retail space to 105,000 square feet." This store, by the way, was the first to incorporate a tree in its interior. The eighty-five-foot tree was designed and built by Nature Makers, a firm that built trees for Disney World. In 2002, another store opened in St. Cloud, Minnesota, at 128,000 square feet. A new store in Omaha, Nebraska, opened in 2004, composed of 177,000 square feet, the first store to incorporate a Ferris wheel. Six months later, SCHEELS 23rd superstore opened in Des Moines, Iowa—2,000 square feet larger.

Imagine this cascade of openings, with each store requiring more and more space to handle the increasing sporting goods inventory that the American culture, as Steve had predicted years before, demanded when sports became a lifestyle, not a mere pastime. Steve's and his teams' creative innovations included in-store games, foods, candies, Ferris wheels, and the rest one might imagine. But the greatest offer of all would not end in a cakewalk.

In 2002, Steve received a call from Mayor Geno Martini of Sparks, Nevada and the Governor of Nevada, Jim Gibbons. "They told me they had done their research and visited our newest stores in Des Moines and Omaha, and would like us to open a store in Sparks, a suburb of Reno. I told them we had no interest, and that's when the negotiations started. They wanted a large retailer to draw customers from California and Oregon who would shop and pay sales tax in Nevada. In 2006, we signed a deal with free land and $40,000,000 in cash to help build the Sparks store."

Included in the plans were two arched 16,000-gallon aquariums, one at each entrance, so customers could walk under the arches that were stocked with brilliantly colored fish—besides an atrium with a 65-foot Ferris wheel. Steve says, "Those aquariums! We had to have someone in each market to take care of them. We'll train them if there isn't someone else, but it's very labor-intensive. With that many fish and aquatic life, and salt-and-fresh water, it's a daily task. We have a place in the back of each store that you don't see where fish are taken out to recuperate or pass away, because you don't want a tank of upside-down fish and have some kid say, 'Dad, look!'"

The store also provided a shooting gallery and sports simulators for customers to test their skills, along with forty-some flavors of fudge served at Grandma Ginna's restaurant, named after Steve's mother.

After investing $60 million of SCHEELS own money, Steve oversaw the construction of the Sparks venue, which at 295,000 square feet would cover the square footage of five-and-a-half football fields. The Sparks store opened at the end of September 2008, a month before the Great Recession hit every economic entity in the U. S., especially real estate—and the hardest hit state in the country was Nevada.

"Our 300,000 square foot store was a huge construction project," Steve says, with the suggestion that this was not his best creative idea, and he was right to resist it at first. "I had no idea how I would pay contractors in 2007 and 2008, when bank after bank refused to

Walk beneath huge aquariums and enjoy living fish of every sort above and on both sides

issue us credit, despite our sterling credit history." Retail sales turned out to be thirty percent below projections in the new Sparks establishment when it opened. The multi-million-dollar investment threatened not only the existence of the Sparks store but the entire interlinked SCHEELS company, committed to such a monumental investment that even their employee retirement plan, as it existed then, had the potential of going under.

Steve says about that time, "I didn't sleep at night. I lost twenty pounds. I had to go to a doctor, take sleeping pills, no help. I didn't know how we were going to pay our contractors, the ones building our Reno store, which was the largest in the U.S. at the time at roughly 300,000 square feet. I got down on my knees at the side of my bed and I prayed at night, and one night when I prayed, I remember the next day Banker's Trust in Des Moines, Iowa, called and said, 'There's no reason we can't loan you money.'

"It was like the world had been lifted off my shoulders, so between Banker's Trust out of Des Moines and Bell Bank in Fargo, we had no trouble paying our contractors in Reno. And I hope we never go through that again!"

ADVERSITY'S DESTINY

The troubling situation of Sparks led to a further Steve D creative innovation. Since the 1980s he had been concerned with what he saw as the company's greatest unresolved dilemma, which had been only increased by the addition of huge new stores—epic employee turnover. In an employee exit interview he conducted, he found that the most common complaint of employees was their "intense dislike of management."

"My dad always called us managers, and one day I walked into his office, and said, 'You know, I think we should be leaders, not managers.' He said, 'Well, what's the difference?' And I said, 'I've been studying this, and leaders really lead people, and teach people what to do, rather than telling them, like we're doing. Managers kind of manage people and processes, and I think we need to lead our people but manage the processes and our inventory.'

"He said, 'Go for it.'

"Somebody once said," Steve continues, to clarify a point, "'Your dad really doesn't like to talk.' I said, 'Nope. He's got other things he'd rather do. He'd rather be working on photography or reading a book and accomplishing something, rather than idle chit-chat. He had a beautiful darkroom in the basement of both our homes, and he wrote and published both *A Search to See* and *A Search to See II*, and he enjoyed teaching and he enjoyed Ansel Adams, Bret Weston, and Bob Byers, all the friends he met doing black-and-white photography, and that was his passion. His friends spoke his language."

Fred B on a photo excursion

The managers were good salespeople, who spoke a knowledgeable language about sporting supplies and products, but not one was trained in leadership. Steve felt that employees didn't like to be fed information by a talker, much less talked down to, and SCHEELS needed to make an about face and become a model in how to lead. For that to happen, management had to receive training in leadership first, in advance of any of the staff. Steve says, "Leadership has to be studied and learned from the very top on down. Everything starts at the top."

Employees should be led, not managed, was his understanding of the newest innovation, and "the ability of the sales staff to deal with customers as individuals is ultimately what distinguishes a retail outlet," to refer to the Gleiter article. He saw that "customer loyalty in an increasingly competitive retail environment would determine the level of SCHEELS success and even its survival," to again quote Gleiter.

Steve explained to his father, Yes, the stores "should be managing processes and important matters like inventory. But we should be leading *people*." Steve had traveled with his father many times between stores, and on these occasions they talked a lot, as Steve recounts. He learned not only precise business organization but was served a portion of family history, which, before Fred B's writing, had not been passed on.

A certain craftiness undergirded the Scheel family verbal reserve, as Steve D points out. "We worked too hard to turn around and tell our competitors what we do. It was a private conversation we had, and it was funny, too, because I can read all those articles laid out on that desk"—a sweep of his arm to a desk farther off—"from the

sporting goods intelligence from the last eight years, and they guess at everything. We didn't tell them anything, and they write a pretty good article about 'Go visit this new store,' but they guess at sales, they guess at what we're doing. Then they talk to our vendors and our vendors tell them what kind of company we are, and that's fun to read because they think they got it right."

Fred B maintained a positive outlook in his writing and photography, and it was perhaps that internal attitude that led to his election as president of the Plains Art Museum in Moorhead. And in 1989, he was appointed Chairman of "Community Day," a celebration of the one hundredth anniversary of North Dakota State University; the next year, 1990, he was awarded an honorary degree, Doctor of Laws, from NDSU. In his "Biographical Calendar" for 1991, a simple straightforward sentence appears: "Son, Steve, elected President and head of the business."

HARD STUDY

Steve began a series of storewide training sessions to establish the sense of leadership he believed was needed to open the stores even wider to customer retail interest. His belief was, "If we can turn out the best leaders in retail, we don't have to worry about the competition." He was now CEO and president, as Fred B confirmed, and was confident that leaders could be taught as well as those who were born to lead. He believed leadership was the key to sewing up complete success at SCHEELS. The relationships his training taught the sales staff to establish with customers resulted in not one layoff or downsizing over the harrowing year of 2008.

The steamboat captain and book publisher, owner of the printing press that ran the biography of Ulysses S. Grant, Mark Twain, said, "The man who does not read holds no advantage over the man who cannot read." More and more readers fall into the oblivion of non-advantage and non-information, imagining they will receive all they need by Googling it. This includes college students enrolled in literature classes. Steve, as leader himself, understood this lack, and became a kind of surrogate reader for the employees. He introduced monthly readings, mandatory ones, for store leaders, from books such as John C. Maxwell's *The 21 Irrefutable Laws of Leadership.*

One of Maxwell's maxims clarified for Steve, at least partly, his own outlook: "Great leaders always seem to embody two seemingly disparate qualities. They are both highly visionary and highly practical."

Although Steve in his creative innovations to retail sales seems to fill both qualifications, he says, "I'm not sure I was so visionary; maybe I was just lucky." Besides those qualities, in reference to the training he was embarking on, he acknowledges the author Tom Peters, who wrote, "Leaders don't create more followers, they create more leaders." That struck home. He knew his father was a leader, but his father's leadership was held in abeyance by tradition and his application of creativity to outside projects.

Steve's readings supplied goals he set for SCHEELS stores over a specific business year, and it became the duty of store leaders to train the more than six hundred *assistant* store leaders by holding weekly meetings at each store. The leaders themselves were to embody the leadership qualities each reading emphasized. Steve prepared the lessons and questions for weekly staff meetings, which the store leaders, as they were now called, conducted at each location. He believed repetition was important. "For every leader at SCHEELS we've got the same quote, the same goal. It's really five parts: 'We take good people; We lead them by example; We immerse them in our culture; We help them become great and continually better at what they do, while helping them enjoy their career or part-time job at SCHEELS.'

"The important part is immersing them in our culture because our culture is significantly different from the culture outside our doors. If we can do that, if they can lead in doing that, we continually teach that, teach that, teach that. I can do my job, but am I leading others by example and encouragement? Culture trumps strategy. Our culture makes us who we are and, yes, we have these strategies for different things we go through, but we live or we die with our leadership and our culture."

This is to say that a vibrant culture has a moralizing effect.

MORAL EFFECT

As suggested by one of Steve's five innovations, a further method of establishing leadership was selective hiring. He knew that absorbing information didn't necessarily translate into treating colleagues or customers as one should. So he set high standards for all employees, focusing on character rather than particular skills per se.

"We hire for attitude and train for skill" was his mantra. Each person has admirable skills, but if a proper attitude is absent that skill might as well not exist. To advance, employees have to go through an evaluation process twice a year. "I do a lot of leadership training still," Steve says, "especially in the key leader positions of maybe twenty-two people, and they hold twenty-six to twenty-seven meetings a year.

"We rank or rate our leadership from Number One, which means they are brand new in their leadership role in a store, to Number Nine, ready to run a SCHEELS store. I don't do the training any more with the Nines and Tens, but we will bring in a group of One, Two, Three, and Fours to Fargo for a week of training."

In the Fargo gathering Steve is often the one who opens the talks, gives attendees an idea of why they are present for the training, and what the expectations of SCHEELS in general and Steve in particular will be. This is one mode of further opening the SCHEELS experience to customers, and an essential of Steve's philosophy is removing any final separating wall between the customer and employee and the customer's retail experience.

Of his attendees, he says, "I give them a challenge at the end; they have to reply to me by a certain date on the part of the challenge they're going to take up. We use five or six textbooks to teach from. I like to say I'm still involved with that. I'm redoing all my leadership lessons right now, because they can be better than they are. I keep telling our people, 'You're either improving or falling behind; there's no coasting.' If you're coasting, you're going downhill, and that's how I think about myself—that same way.

"One thing I've always done, I've always criticized myself. If I gave a speech like the Lincoln Economic Development in Lincoln, or at the Leadership Institute here in Fargo, I always say when the door closes, 'What could I have done better?' I go over those moments and write that in. And when I coached the kids in Moorhead in hockey, I used to say to myself, 'Next practice I can do this better.'" That comes naturally to me. It doesn't come naturally for a lot of people. I feel I'm the Ambassador for SCHEELS, I'm the head cheerleader for SCHEELS. I kick off our leadership meetings and I participate in our board meetings."

For a person of faith who is a professional in business, it's clear that no neutrality exists. Shoplifting and price fixing are both crimes. A person is either moving toward what is right and good, toward increased virtue, or away from it. There is no middle ground, no standing still, no settling in one spot. Whether it's in business or politics or social matters or the culture, a person has to be moving toward the good, the positive side of the moral spectrum. That is why the Scheel family is involved in the church.

FURTHER EFFECTS

Steve D further explains, "My wife and I are *very* involved. In fact we left a church that had a pretty liberal set of professor-pastors who preached a couple of sermons condemning capitalists. So I sat down and had a conversation with the two and said, 'If this happens again—' Well, we're one of the biggest supporters because I believe in supporting the church, but we were out of there. We went back to First Lutheran in Fargo, where I was baptized and confirmed, and they welcomed us with open arms.

"We are involved with many aspects of First Lutheran Church, especially with mission trips my wife will never go on, but I enjoy. I enjoy sleeping in a hammock between two trees without any electricity in Chiapas, Mexico, and I'm happy to support First Lutheran in their missionary work and their youth programs. We contribute to Dollars for Scholars, yes, and my wife and I have started some Friends of the Children chapters.

"Friends of the Children is a unique charity started by Duncan Campbell in Seattle, Washington. He started one in Fargo that we helped fund and we started one in Missoula, Montana, and got our Missoula manager on the board. We started one in Colorado Springs, with our Colorado Springs manager on the board to make sure things are going well. But what 'Friends' do is first they train with the Koch Foundation in Wichita, where they learn how to run a business.

"We found that most people in a charity have a big heart but don't have much business sense. So we send each local Executive Director of Friends of the Children to the Koch Foundation to learn how to run a charity, and then the Koch Foundation teaches them, manages them, and every single month monitors their financial statement. Then they go to the Friends of the Children in Seattle and learn how to run a Friends of the Children chapter, and then come back to Fargo or wherever, and we give them an office and they hire a Friend, and that Friend is paid about $55,000 a year, and that Friend has to take six foster children, six four- or five-year-old children, and take care of them until they graduate from high school.

"So they have a steady influence in their lives, rather than going from foster home to foster home, but now a Friend in Fargo, in Missoula, Colorado Springs, will take six of those kids. Right now we have four Friends in Fargo, so actually there are twenty-four kids in Fargo who have a Friend. They have to spend I think a minimum of six hours a week with each child, meaning Friends spend at least thirty-six hours a week to help with homework, or take the kids to sporting events, or whatever, so their 'Friend' becomes a constant in their lives.

"Eileen and I had a meeting with Duncan Campbell who started this, and we jumped on board because I think it's a fantastic program. People don't have to worry about how their money is being spent because the Koch Foundation monitors it with an iron hand out of Wichita, and we get reports on a regular basis. We work with them.

"Eileen helped lead a Jeremiah Project here in town—she got that going, she and her friend Sandra got that going, and it's fun to be involved. We've been blessed. We give back both time and financially to keep things going." In this way, Steve and Eileen have given a monumental philanthropic offering to the University of Mary as lead donors of the Crow's Nest Campus Restaurant.

When the administrators at the University of Mary began looking forward to a central campus location and food service, they decided against a cafeteria-style installation, where students line up for a helping of this and a helping of that and dispense their own drink, and that is it. No, the Crow's Nest has been a gathering space since 2017 of restaurant-level food choices nestled at the center of the university, in the *Lumen Vitae*—The Light of Life— University Center.

The Crow's Nest offers several separate serving areas that provide an array of food choices, including soup-and-salad, make-your-own sandwich, home-cooked, grilled, Italian, non-gluten and special diet, and Mongolian grilled—a student favorite. The Crow's Nest is the ideal gathering place for students, faculty, and staff, open twenty-four seven with its wide variety of foods and pool tables and a dozen large display screens for viewing all types of sports.

That is the essence of leadership in the church and in Christian outreach that Steve and Eileen Scheel choose to be involved in at the present.

CAPTURE CULTURE

Under the training Steve D and other SCHEELS leaders established and continue to address, the leadership team at each store is responsible for that store—for the hiring, the managing of orders, and all systems that focus on increasing local revenue by introducing customers to a creative matrix where they're served by employees that SCHEELS has trained for the moment. Each store is run nearly entirely in-house rather than by an overseeing computer or face-time distance. This enables store leaders and salespeople to remain local and establish relationships with local customers.

In a final intimate touch instituted by Fred M, SCHEELS asks employees to wear not only name tags but below that the name of their hometown—a further means of removing the wall between employees and customers by encouraging conversation. The turnover of full-time employees at all SCHEELS stores across the board has reached the lowest level in the industry, down to sixteen percent from eighteen percent last year, and the turnovers usually happen within the first year or two of employees being hired.

The bottom line to Steve is to bear foremost in mind that employees are creations of God with dignity, never merely company assets. "When I listen to a concern employees have about the business or their home lives," Steve said, "I ask a few questions. Then I can help them become a better person at SCHEELS. Trust is the bedrock of leadership." He teaches leaders to become leaders by getting to know an employee, "asking about hobbies, knowing the name of their

Steve and Eileen receive framed gratitude from Monsignor James Shea for funding of the Crow's Nest

spouses and children and finding out what's going on in their lives. And it's important for leaders, when at their duties on a floor, to smile at employees and always acknowledge a job well done."

He upholds and exemplifies that approach as the essence of SCHEELS corporate culture, and walks the floor himself to express the joyous gravity of servant leadership he hopes to instill in those employed at SCHEELS.

FURTHER FIX

Hasn't everybody walked into a big-box or building-supply-plumbing-electrical store and found it necessary to search for a salesperson and when at last you've found one and ask where you can locate x-and-x, you hear, "Gee, I'm not sure," or "Let me see if I can find my manager." Only the truly patient—or desperate—customer will tolerate this too many times. In the same way that Steve created the innovative leadership training, he added a training system to guarantee SCHEELS had the best-informed staff in retail sales.

After studying the Odyssey Company in Japan, SCHEELS established the *Scheels University System*, which is located in Sioux Falls and Fargo. Most of the training in sport and outdoor clothes and footwear and running gear takes place in Fargo, while other training occurs in Sioux Falls. This is to ensure that all innovative training that SCHEELS has established will be carried out as it was first pictured in the leadership's imagination.

A sales member will spend a week at the appropriate training center or, in certain cases, at several of them. Each person is tested on his or her product knowledge when they enter a facility. During the week's study of products, staff members are introduced to instructors from Trek Bicycle, for instance—SCHEELS the top dealer of Trek Bicycle in the world.

The staff might also be instructed by a representative from a golf company, who demonstrates how to use products properly, so staff is able to not only talk about the products but illustrate their use. When the week is over a final exam is administered and each staff member must retain, at minimum, ninety-five percent knowledge on all products demonstrated or explained to them. If any of the staff scores lower than ninety-five percent, that person will not be authorized to sell those products for SCHEELS. The ability to handle on-floor sales properly is that important to SCHEELS—a result of its urge for excellence in the retail experience. As the motto at the foot of Steve Scheel's stationery has it: "Our goal is to be the best retailer in the USA in the eyes and minds of our customers and our associates."

BIG BENEFITS

After this training, why shouldn't store leaders and employees share in the profits of SCHEELS as it expands across the U.S.? Once SCHEELS was established as an all-sports retail chain, their hardware sales over except for Southside Fargo, Steve turned to his dad and the two worked out a way to convert the family-and-management-owned company into an employee-owned corporation by establishing an Employee Stock Ownership Plan (ESOP). Steve and Fred B hoped to acknowledge any sacrifices SCHEELS employees might make and to reward their efforts by assuring them they would be able to retire comfortably.

The ESOP graciously enrolls beginning employees who can become shareholders at the age of twenty-one. The entry level is available to anybody who works one thousand hours in one year, which means twenty-five weeks or one-half-year of forty-hour-a-week employment. Employees enrolled in ESOP undergo an attitude change from generally ho-hum, say, that a worker might have, into being part-owner of SCHEELS. Now they're involved in the business in a new way, as Fred B and Steve D foresaw.

And the best part, as he sees it, is that ESOP enables employees to retire with a larger package than most retirement plans can establish. "We just had a young woman retire whose ESOP payment was millions. And her husband, who threatened to leave about forty years ago, I convinced to stay. He gave me his letter of resignation, sitting right there in my office, and I took one look at it and ripped it up, threw it in the trash, said, 'You're stupid to leave.' He stayed on and doubled what his wife received, went out and bought a huge tract of shoreline, and is building a place for himself, for his grandkids.

"He and his wife were the greatest people, and it was fun to see them able to do whatever they want. A cashier who retired had a nice check and she came to my office door—*knock! knock!*—the door is always open, and I looked up and it was Katy, let's call her, and she had tears in her eyes, and said, 'Can I give you a hug?' And I said, 'Well, Katy, you're not employed here anymore, so it will not be sexual harassment!' We gave each other a hug, and she said, 'We just bought the lake home of our dreams, and we still have half of our ESOP left.' Boy, does that make you feel good!

"The amount we have to set aside to cover these checks has increased substantially, and that's our first priority as far as maintaining cash. A lot of ESOPs struggle because it's an unfunded liability, and you don't have a separate account where you have cash tucked away to pay for it. In order to have a way to pay people, your operation has to generate enough cash each year to first take care of your retirees and ESOP, and then do any expansion or remodel or capital improvements.

"We've always maintained that the employee who's going to retire is the first priority, so our CFO and her team do a kind of projection on what we'll need every year, and we want to make sure we've got cash way in excess of that plan coming from operations. We have no trouble taking care of those people, and that's one of the biggest thrills I have. I write a separate note to every ESOP retiree, thanking them, wishing them the best, and a lot of us stay in contact even after they leave. I enjoy it when I get an email or they want to walk into the office and say, 'Thank you.' And I say 'I have to thank you because you helped build our company!'

GENEROSITY'S GIFT

"And now—now we're basically debt-free. We don't owe anybody any money. We can do whatever we want, and we'll build new stores."

It's the creative innovations initiated by Steve D and others that brought about this change in business, after the near-failure of 2008. He says, "Our current stores generate the cash we need to build the stores. And you sleep real well at night because bankers can't tell you what to do. You can do exactly what you want to do, when you want to do it, and we've got such a great team. I look at the team, and we've got a *new* Store Development Team led by a fellow who started part-time, selling shoes at Grand Forks when he went to UND. Now he's our VP of New Store Development. He builds our new stores; he does all the remodels, and I watch what he's doing here with my new office and I'm just in awe that we took this kid, selling shoes part-time, who had kind of a knack for construction. Now he's full-time Vice President.

"He used to be the marketing leader as well for Sarah Moseng, an assistant leader, but he was interested in so much we also had him leading New Store Development while leading the marketing department."

Steve understood the situation and the special nature of the young man's gifts with a sense of discernment he has for those who will work out for SCHEELS and those who won't, and is not afraid to admit his errors when they occur. "Sarah almost quit when we woke up to the fact that, no, this was too much for Jason.

"Sarah is our wonderful assistant marketing leader, so she has a team that works under her, and I can't keep track of all they do. The marketing VP over there in that other corporate building has a great team of seven assistant leaders in marketing, and Sarah is one of the keys that helps lead the events we put on. If she wasn't real sharp, she wouldn't be in that position. That's what we do. We try people, and usually we're fairly confident because of their past and their work ethic and attitude. They can learn to handle the position, but if they can't, we have to say, 'This isn't working, and we'll put you somewhere else, because what's best for you is best for any you lead.'"

LARGE LIVES

The ESOP is tied to SCHEELS low turnover rate, and the potential for a lower- or middle-class person, as present-day culture would define that person with condescension, to be able to retire with millions in hand in their mid-fifties—"I'm heading for Santa Fe!"— is the sort of golden parachute that only upper management receives from most major corporations.

The ESOP, however, can grow only as SCHEELS prospers, and a growing government deficit and the highest inflation rate in thirty years, beginning in 2021, can cause any company's profits to wane. But SCHEELS gained traction in the worst recent recession of 2008, and continues, through the sustaining principles of its founding family, to remain true to giving back to employees and the community—a hallmark of immigrants who have benefited from constitutionally guaranteed freedoms, including economic advancement, that the U.S. provides above every other country.

SCHEELS is further committed to a form of community gratitude in a direct manner; every SCHEELS store is required to donate five percent of its profits to local charities and non-profit organizations, and in good years, the donations double out of gratitude, as mentioned. In addition, the Scheels Foundation donates over five million a year to communities, through the local stores.

When one gives, it is given back, according to the gospel of Luke, the container shaken down, overflowing, and set down with greater measure in one's lap. The Scheel family motto, as Fred B passed it to Steve: *change is good.* Innovation that is partner to risk achieves gracious returns, as Steve's example proves. A litany of the stores added is voiced by Steve over the latter part of a video of Scheel family history. "On September 29, 2017, SCHEELS opened a 250,000-square-foot store in Johnstown, Colorado. A store of the same size opened in Lincoln, Nebraska, in 2018. And then a further store in Colorado Springs. In 2019 a new SCHEELS of 240,000 square feet opened in Eden Prairie, Minnesota. And near Dallas, in The Colony, Texas, a new SCHEELS opened in 2020, at 330,000 square feet the largest of its kind for a sporting goods store…"

Yes, an even larger store than the Sparks-Reno near-disaster was put in place recently in The Colony, Texas. This is the Warren Buffet connection. According to a print issue of sportsinsightmag.com for

One of the bowling alleys provided for customer entertainment at SCHEELS

May 2018, "When it opens in spring 2020, Dallas residents will have three choices—Academy Sports + Outdoors, Dick's Sporting Goods and the new SCHEELS.

"The Colony location, which will feature a 65-foot Ferris wheel and 16,000 gallon saltwater aquarium, began construction in February and will eventually employ more than 400 people.

"The store is located in The Colony's $1.5 billion Grandscape development, a project of developer Warren Buffet's Berkshire Hathaway. Some observers have posed the question of whether Buffet's involvement as landlord in the development portends a closer relationship with the family-owned Scheels." Steve D denies that will ever be the case.

The article continues, "'This outfit is my kind of business, with organic growth created by being simply the best retailer in their category,' Buffet said in promoting the partnership. 'The Scheels experience will bring millions of visitors to Grandscape.'" Steve D adds, "Dallas is 330,000 square feet, and that would be ten percent bigger than Reno. Warren Buffet and his team said, 'It's going to be your biggest store ever'—so it's 330 over Reno's 300.

"Our store leader in Texas, who is really good—he's on our board—he says, 'Not big enough. Got to have a warehouse pretty soon—going to have to warehouse off-floor-sales kayaks. They take a lot of space. Bikes, too.'

"Every store, like the new Dallas store, has a store leader and from five to twenty-eight assistant store leaders. Every one of those assistant store leaders leads about eight or nine key people, and the development of those key people is dependent on that assistant store leader. If they can't lead those people, if they can't help those people grow in their careers, we have a problem. The problem is if we put people in place and they don't understand how to lead people and help those they lead to enjoy their work—that's where that five-part quote I mentioned comes into play. With proper leadership, they will become immersed in our culture and find the better person and associate they can be."

A further encouragement is the generous retirement. Steve notes, "Last year our ESOP had a sixty-one percent gain. OK, when an associate has a $100,000 or $200,000 ESOP, and the people designated by the Federal Government to put a value on your ESOP come up with a sixty-one percent gain—wow! When we have that kind of gain and our associates get their ESOP statement, you should see the smiles. Last year I signed one-hundred-eighty-seven ESOP statements for participants who had over $250,000 in their ESOP with that sixty-one percent gain. Think of when they take that home to their spouse, or if they're a couple working for us, they both get that. It makes them feel so good.

"Only certain companies are allowed to put a value on their ESOP, and they rate us against all our retail competitors and look at what kind of year they had, and what kind of year we had. Then they look at all our numbers, look at projections, and they put a value out there, and basically you have to accept it. Because if the government didn't have only approved companies valuing ESOP, and owners like us, in some cases companies would keep chintzing it down and keeping more for themselves and less for their employees, so thank goodness they have to do this.

"Employees can also take hardship distributions, where they look at their ESOP and by law they say, 'We're having problems here, we're having problems there,' and as a company we're able to approve a hardship distribution; they can take something out. But *really*, the way our ESOP is growing, it's much better for them to go get a loan at the bank for seven or even eight percent, than take anything from their ESOP. It's going to grow fifteen to eighteen percent or more this year."

GIFT GIVING

"In our business, no, no, we don't want surplus inventory. We try not to carry anything over because fads change, colors change, sizes change, and we used to sell it, get rid of it, whatever it takes. But now it's ridiculous, because our stores and our volume have gotten so large that at the end of a season, we'll pack up our downhill skis, we'll have a pre-season sale next year. We'll set up our shop, and they're all on sale.

"One thing a lot of our stores do right now when Christmas giving is going on, is first of all we give away our donation checks in December to all the communities. And then at the coat drives, the shoe drives we donate a lot of, well, it may just be a beautiful Nike shoe that's not selling, and we donate those to charities in town. To schools we give backpacks, thousands and thousands of backpacks, and it becomes a time of giving."

And then payroll checks are issued to 9,547 employees, some of whom will claim part of their accumulated ESOP earnings that year.

The former partner-manager Jan Hook adds, "Consistent with Scheels' commitment to autonomy and helping associates grow to be their best, Scheels has, in the ESOP retirement plan, a gift to the associates which is available in very few companies. Over the last ten years, if I have said it once, I have said it one thousand times: Scheels creates more millionaires per capita than any other organization in the U.S. that has a minimum of one hundred employees. I hope that continues for the next one-hundred-twenty years."

A further element to SCHEELS success occurred over Thanksgiving of 2021, when the company ran a televised ad picturing a family of all ages gathering to celebrate, with this voice-over by Steve: "SCHEELS is grateful for our customers, communities, and fellow associates. On Thanksgiving Day, we encourage time with loved ones by closing our doors. And on this day we open our hearts and bow our heads to pray and give thanks—[the family gathers at a table, holding hands, heads bowed]. With grateful hearts, we praise GOD for family and friends, for health and freedom, and for the rich blessing that we enjoy every day. Have a blessed Thanksgiving from all of us at SCHEELS."

This was followed soon by "MERRY CHRISTMAS from all of us at SCHEELS. Our stores are closed today, December 25. All our employees will be celebrating Christmas Day with their families.

"CHRIST IS BORN. 'For unto you is born this day in the city of David a Savior, who is Christ the Lord.' Luke 2:11

"Christmas is a time to pause, reflect and be grateful for the blessings of all who support and guide us like our family, friends, and neighbors. Thank you for finding ways to show kindness and care for one another whether together or apart. From all of us at Scheels, we wish you a blessed and Merry Christmas!"

This outreach into communities in a salutary Christian manner may well be, in the end, an ultimate reason for the enduring success of Scheels. One of the higher-up employees who's been with Scheels for twenty years, who dresses in such stylish clothes she could be in *Vogue*, said, "It's a pleasure to be working for a company that's open about its faith." And it is indeed faith that has kept the Scheel family and, in proper providential sequence, the family business in a unity that has rendered both sides of the equation exceptionally strong. Out of that passionate unity the reality that has emerged is a modern, state-of-the-art retail world.

Once more, Jan Hook: "Finally, perhaps the most important lesson I learned from SCHEELS is the act of giving. Charity is engulfed in SCHEELS culture. Being associated with SCHEELS has eternally engrained the sense of charity in my life. SCHEELS is far more than a business success story or a legacy of any sort. SCHEELS is a historical process of improving the lives of innumerable people inside and outside the parameters of the business. Nothing can be said about any business which is more significant than that."

SCHEELS LOCATIONS

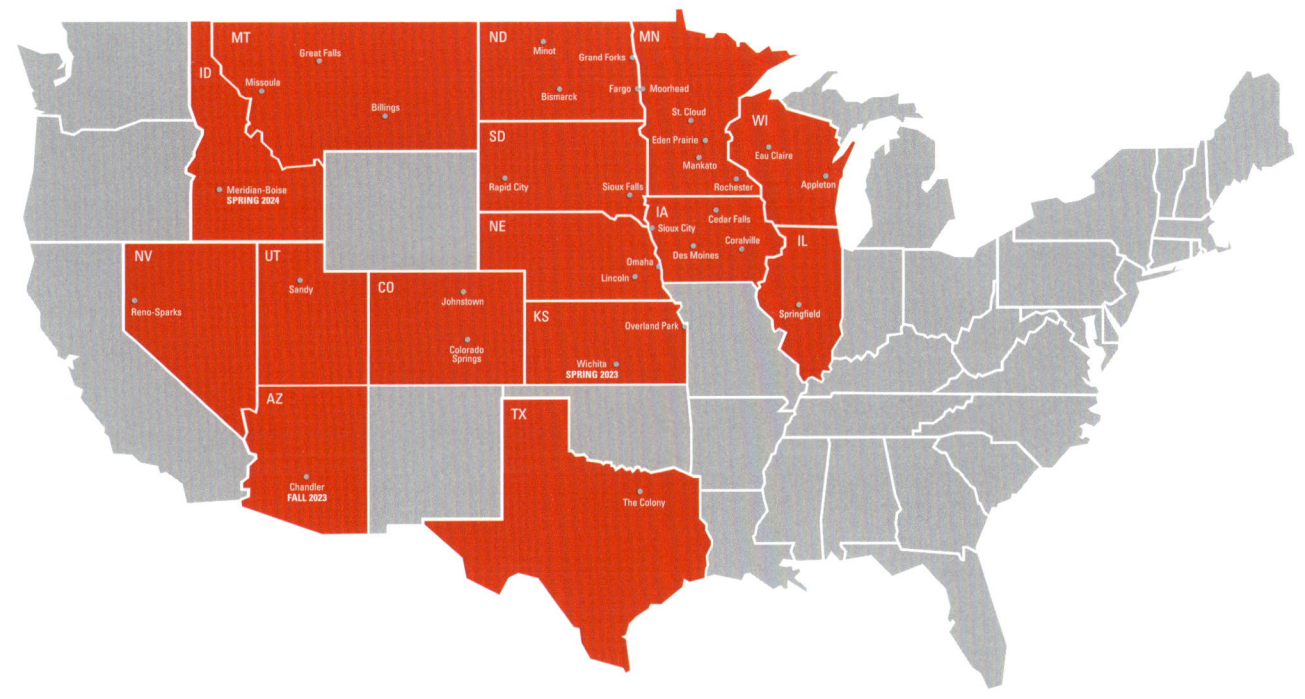

Map of the United States with highlighted states and city locations:

- **MT**: Great Falls, Missoula, Billings
- **ID**: Meridian-Boise SPRING 2024
- **ND**: Minot, Grand Forks, Fargo, Bismarck
- **MN**: Moorhead, St. Cloud, Eden Prairie, Mankato, Rochester
- **WI**: Eau Claire, Appleton
- **SD**: Rapid City, Sioux Falls
- **IA**: Sioux City, Cedar Falls, Coralville, Des Moines
- **NE**: Omaha, Lincoln
- **IL**: Springfield
- **NV**: Reno-Sparks
- **UT**: Sandy
- **CO**: Johnstown, Colorado Springs
- **KS**: Overland Park, Wichita SPRING 2023
- **AZ**: Chandler FALL 2023
- **TX**: The Colony

ADDENDUM

AN INTRODUCTION

The following essay serves as creative credo for Frederick B Scheel. It appears in the opening pages of *A Search To See II* and is titled "About Photography." It is uncompromising in its view of the value of previous generations, while at the same maintaining independence in any cultural artistic outlook. He writes, "I try to maintain my own independence of vision as steadfastly as any other primary principle by which I live. Today's constant hammering by critics and commentators would shape us all into their molds or confuse us so we lose confidence…"

An early point is that no matter how fruitful the material our five senses deliver to us, "information is hardly enough to make life the chariot of wonders it can be…" and "we sometimes need the fuel of fiction for a flight of fantasy, plus an itinerary of thought and intuition to enhance our travels of the mind." And then he refers to the sentences that stand as epigraph to this book: "Thought, fantasy, intuition, all are priceless heirlooms surviving countless generations. They provide no simple map, but rather a chart of finest tapestry, woven with threads of empirical wisdom by a thousand family weavers who walked before."

The work of the creative artist, the photographer in particular, is to enter that weave of wisdom and "to set forth what few may have seen but which many, once shown, will recognize." He affirms, "I have no social message to convey in my photography except my overriding belief in the dignity of man everywhere."

The recognition of truly original creative art "invites the mind on a journey from some radiant chapter in its past, along the winding road of intuition, into an unknown yet recognizable land beyond."

In that "unknown yet recognizable land beyond," he affirms a faith he emphasizes in holding to a vision "as steadfastly as any other primary principle by which I live." This steadfast vision is the result of generational faith, further increased by Fred B's passion for nature, and is the bright beauty shining from creation at the still center of the revolving universe.

[A sense of the complexity of the collection is revealed in its dedication]

Brett Weston

Who, more than all others, taught me to see through all those wonder-filled days and weeks in the field, and through many evenings viewing and discussing photographs.

Virginia, my wife,

For her companionship and her seeing on hundreds of thousands of miles of roaming North America, Europe, Africa, and islands, and her thousands of evenings spent alone while I worked in the darkroom.

Ansel Adams and Robert Byers

For the introductions to serious photography and photographers.

And Mother and Dad

Who planted the seed and cultivated the tree those many years before it began to bear fruit.

Joseph and Charles Gagon
Riviére-Quelle, Gaspé, 1976

ABOUT
PHOTOGRAPHY

Each of us has tools enough to sustain our exploration of life, its origins, its course, its destiny beyond our allotted years. Through our eyes and ears, nose, tongue, and sense of touch flow rivers of information to the mind. But information is hardly enough to make life the chariot of wonders it can be. Rather than a forest of facts, we sometimes need the fuel of fiction for a flight of fantasy, plus an itinerary of thought and intuition to enhance our travels of the mind.

Thought, fantasy, intuition, all are priceless heirlooms surviving countless generations. They provide no simple map, but rather a chart of finest tapestry, woven with threads of empirical wisdom by a thousand family weavers who walked before. From such treasure charts the photographer finds his way, to set forth what few may have seen but which many, once shown, will recognize. And so we search for such a photograph. It will not be one that conveys only information through the river of the eye, nor is it solely an emanation of the mind. Rather, it will be a visual revelation that invites the mind on a journey from some radiant chapter in its past, along the winding road of intuition, into an unknown yet recognizable land beyond. If the photograph says too much, there is no mystery, and the mind dismisses the invitation. Photographs with all content revealed, every thicket bared, tend to say too much. With no mystery they wait in vain. Or they may say too little, or nothing. No siren calls. The viewer moves on.

Yet, if that primeval chord no mortal has yet defined is struck, then we respond. We linger, as if in a spell, for seconds, or a laden minute, or, for that rare photograph, even longer. Occasionally, we return, lured back by a master's, or on rare occasions a novice's, radiant visual refrain.

A good photograph, like the worthy invention or valued writing, is rarely a lucky apple dropped from the tree of fortune. Most result from energy and perseverance, organized application and search. Honesty also plays a role as does time, to help distill the best. We needn't fight those in which we yet find no treasured thread, but know that honesty is needed to avert sham in extolling, or even accepting, such until we do. Four hundred years ago, Shakespeare had Polonius counsel "To thine own self be true." Nowhere is that advice more relevant than in art, and, as a consequence, in photography.

I try to maintain my own independence of vision as steadfastly as any other primary principle by which I live. Today's constant hammering by critics and commentators would shape us all into their molds or confuse us so we lose confidence in our own eye. A study of the history of art reveals that critics have been about as often wrong as right, no matter the age or the art reviewed. Edward Weston was at least partly correct when he complained, "The only thing critics do is psychoanalyze themselves." Further, honing one's own vision enables us to enjoy many aspects of art beyond the genre studied: paintings, sculpture, architecture, design, decorating, nature… wherever we look.

My dominant purpose is to make a photograph which appeals to my own critical senses; not only appeals but so stimulates as to make the reward greater than the considerable effort, time and discipline expended.

Daily, as I look out upon the world, I must ask myself, "What do I see?" in "ODE ON INTIMATIONS OF IMMORTALITY," William Wordsworth wrote, "The things which I have seen I now can see no more." But the photographer must seek and find ways of revealing that which others "now can see no more." The goal, the success, is in making the photograph that carries the viewer back through the halls, perhaps even some remote, dim passageway, of his heritage.

Photographs vary as much as food and tastes do, and for many of the same reasons. Strong among the reasons are the corridors built or traveled through by our ancestors, complemented by more recent hallways designed and decorated by our personal study and experience.

I work in two ways: by making compositions in my own studio, or by photographing out in the field, driving through villages and countrysides, or walking the streets of towns and cities. I'm not sure which is more, or less, productive. Two or three weeks in the field can fail to yield one worthwhile image—and often does. And a half dozen two to three-hour sessions in the studio may be just as fruitless.

In the field I may have available more than a hundred compositions each hour, whereas in the studio there may be a half dozen in the same period. Making one's own compositions can be frustrating, and is perhaps why Renoir said, "I work to fashion a satisfactory floral arrangement… and then turn it around and paint it from the other side."

The ease of operating modern cameras increases the eagerness to make too many photographs but, too few that are well thought out. It is one disadvantage of the medium. Remember: Each master photographer, great painter, writer, or composer is best known for his or her ten or fewer most famous works. Quantity is not the goal. But quantity is almost universally necessary for distilling the significant final few in any field of creation or invention.

For portraits I look for a strong face and poise before the camera. The character that radiates from and the stature that distinguishes a few otherwise humble people when before the camera can be magnificent.

Good photographs do not come in flocks. One, maybe two, in a year can deem that period a success. The first photograph of mine which I saw in aesthetic terms was Dawn Over the Vermillion Lakes, Banff, which I made in 1951 at the age of thirty. The next was Boxelder Grove, selected by Ansel Adams in 1961 for APERTURE, and the third, General Store, Jackson, Louisiana in 1966. These were made years apart.

I have not been able to define or even approach a formula for a good photograph, which just seems to happen, or fail to happen, most of the time. Many which I excitedly anticipate to be exceptional, and of which I make three or four or more exposures, become nothings. But others, which seemed less promising, became images of a lifetime, although I had made only one exposure. Why? I don't know. Each year of experience enables one to become more discerning, but a question always remains about the final strength of a photograph until printed and hung on the wall in good light.

Too often I see only what I expect to see rather than all that is truly there. Or I see what I expect to see even if it is not there. Surely, how we see is also tempered by the experiences of our vision prior to selecting the subject and composition and making the final exposure, much as the taste of wine by food or drink consumed immediately before it.

In a new land, or when we walk through "gates" into new worlds opened to us by inspiring art, our vision is heightened, we see more acutely, if only briefly. If I have not been inspired or moved by a work, my own or another's, to me it is not art. Conversely, if I have, it is. This does not mean that the work is not art just because I do not respond to it, but it is not art for me…yet.

I have no social message to convey in my photography except my overriding belief in the dignity of man everywhere. I do feel a dislike approaching disgust for photographs degrading mankind. There is enough agony in the world that the portraying of it, other than to correct it, is a blight in itself. We need, instead, to be inspired by revelations of joy, or perseverance and endurance, of courage, of beauty.

If you have not already purchased photographs but are considering doing so, I would strongly encourage you. Nothing else is likely to teach you to see as well as the commitment to select a purchase, and own good photographs and then to study and enjoy them once they are up on your walls in good light. Because no one else has your particular combination of intuition and experience etched upon his personal vision, only you can select the photograph that most pleases you. You may welcome counsel, but do not rely upon it exclusively. It is better to make a mistake in your selection than to purchase a photograph you do not like for reasons you do not understand.

Whatever your goal in photography, realize that this is an inexhaustible field. Beginning early in life or late, the serious student of this rich discipline will be more than rewarded for his or her application of mind, talent, energy, and will.

Some practices or considerations I have found worthwhile:

- I make only a couple prints of one image the first time I print it.

- Then I wait until the next day or even later, when I have a fresh vision, to study those made earlier before I continue.

- I try to dispense with marginal or weaker photographs at once to free more time to work on the best.

- The best photographs have pasture enough for the imagination.

Sunflower
North Dakota, 1991

UNIVERSITY *of* MARY PRESS